Outwitting Mice
and Other Rodents

Outwitting Mice and Other Rodents

Bill Adler Jr.

The Lyons Press

copyright © 2001 by Adler and Robin Books, Inc.

Printed in Canada

10 9 8 7 6 5 4 3 2 1

Library of Congress Cataloging-in-Publication Data is available on file.

Contents

Introduction

*H*ate is a very strong word. What the average homeowner and gardener feels toward more common rodents, such as the house mouse, roof rat, squirrel, and chipmunk, is not hate, rather it is a combination of fear and loathing. People who make it their mission to rid their homes and lives of rodents are often perceived as evil animal haters motivated by hatred who seek to wipe out vast rodent populations. That couldn't be further from the truth (although I'm sure it is in some cases). For the most part we have no problem sharing this beautiful world with all of its creatures. Just because we are larger and our intelligence cannot be rivaled does not mean we, alone, should benefit from nature. It's just that we would rather not share our personal belongings, such as breakfast cereals or last night's casserole, with creatures that spend their free time rifling through Dumpsters. The bottom drawer of the bureau is meant for socks only, not to house a house mouse. We plant vegetables and fruit trees so that we can cut down on purchasing overpriced produce, not to feed neighborhood creatures.

It takes a long time for most people to get to the point where they are masterminding the demise of certain pests. Whether it is the persistent mouse in your cupboard, or the squirrel targeting your bird feeder, eventually something will send you over the edge. But once you get to that point you have to make sure you are fully prepared, that you are up to the challenge. Just remember to keep your wits when outwitting rodents. You'll need them.

1

Rodents in the United States

Human beings are surrounded by rodents daily—and most of the time we are not aware of it. This statement does not apply to the millions of Americans who are plagued with rodent infestations in their homes and yards. Most likely those people have a good idea what creature is running behind their walls and scurrying past their feet. But with the exception of mice and rats and a few other members of the order Rodentia, few people can identify the less outgoing and bold rodents. It's often difficult to determine which critter bears the mark of a rodent. One of the most common misconceptions is that if it's small, hairy, has whiskers, a long tail, and beady eyes, then you have identified your suspect. Yes, many of those traits are characteristic of rodents, but that's only part of the picture. Since rodents come in a variety of sizes and shapes it usually takes getting up close and personal—examining the animal's teeth—to determine, first, if it is a rodent, and second, to which species it belongs.

Determining its species is key, because there is no panacea for a rodent problem. The remedy has to be specially crafted to suit the critter.

Since the goal is to outwit and outsmart the creatures wreaking havoc in your gardens and homes, you must delve into their lives and minds, just as they invade your property. Albeit a terrifying task, you must learn to think and operate like a rodent.

How They Got Here

Rodents might be new to you, but the world is not new to rodents. Rodents can be traced back nearly sixty million years ago to North America, with the earliest fossilized remains resembling the modern day squirrel, according to some sources. The origin of rodents is the subject of much debate, and their history is a difficult one to follow due to several factors, including their size. Being petite meant that they were easy prey for larger animals that were able to consume them in their entirety, leaving relatively little (such as bones) behind to be used as evidence of their existence. Despite the lack of fossil evidence, scientists used other means, such as rodents' teeth, to trace the evolution of rodents. Experts are able to deduce from the high incidence of teeth sightings that during the Tertiary period, twenty-six to sixty-six million years ago, the rodent population was on the rise—and a steep rise at that.

Leading the evolution of rodents is the squirrel, whose remains were first sighted in North America during the Eocene period, between fifty-four and thirty-seven million years ago. During the following epoch, the Oligocene period, about twenty-three to thirty-eight million years ago, pocket gophers and beavers joined the squirrels, making their North American debut. The end of the Oligocene period proved to be prolific, as the variety of the rodent population seemed to increase worldwide. But it was not until the Pliocene era, two to five million years ago, that the inaugural rats and mice scurried onto the scene.

After millions of years of dating and mating, there are roughly two thousand species of rodents, accounting for 40 percent of the global mammalian population. Very adaptable creatures, mice can be found on every continent except Antarctica. Rodents did not travel around the world without some assistance, however. They had help, *our* help. Human beings must take responsibility for the impressive distribution of some rodents. Where there were ships, there were mice. And wherever the ships arrived, the mice found a new home. (Early European pioneers inadvertently transported Old World mice from Europe to North America via ships.)

This table illustrates the most common rodents in the six regions of the United States. From the looks of these rodent demographics, the farther west you live, the better off you are. But if you think variety is the spice of life, you'll feel right at home in New England and the Mid-Atlantic.

New England	Deer mice, Norway rats, roof rats, muskrat, voles, gray squirrels, chipmunks, red squirrels, porcupines, groundhogs
Mid-Atlantic Region	Deer mice, Norway rats, roof rats, muskrats, beavers, gray squirrels, chipmunks
The South	Norway rats, roof rats, muskrats, beavers, squirrels, chipmunks
The Midwest	Deer mice, Norway rats, muskrats, beavers, prairie dogs, voles, porcupines, gophers
Southwest	Deer mice, Norway rats, prairie dogs, voles, porcupines, gophers
Pacific Northwest	Deer mice, Norway rats, roof rats, muskrats, beavers, voles, lemmings
West Coast	Deer mice, Norway rats, roof rats, voles, porcupines

Why Rodents Exist

Rodents were put on earth for one thing—to gnaw. They are best known for gnawing on (and destroying) anything in their paths. The list of objects they enjoy sinking their teeth into seems endless—food, wiring, cardboard boxes, plastic bags, wood. The term rodent is derived from the Latin word *rodere,* which means to gnaw. With that in mind, it should come as no surprise that the identifying characteristic of rodents is their dentition, or teeth. Their teeth are designed to hack away at food sources otherwise inaccessible by other mammals.

Despite the diversity among rodents, they all have the same dental pattern: a pair of large, powerful, sharp incisors on both the upper and lower jaws and a few pairs of molars. With the exception of a few species, most rodents have twenty-two teeth or fewer. The upper incisors are more pronounced and are more curved than the lower ones, but both sets meet at one point, creating a sharp cutting edge. To their benefit and our general misfortune, gnawing keeps their front teeth small and sharp, making them increasingly effective tools for their trade.

Usually there are three pairs of molars, which grind food so that it can be swallowed. Molars vary from rodent to rodent, which is useful in distinguishing one from another. A rodent's diet can be harsh on molars and incisors. Regularly chewing on seeds, bark, and vegetation can grate on their teeth, sometimes causing damage that could seriously inhibit their ability to chew and digest food. But rodents have evolved so that their teeth grow throughout the animal's life.

There is a vacant space between the incisors and the molars known as the diastema. This gap enables the rodent to pull in its cheeks behind the incisors, so that it can gnaw while simultaneously swallowing other materials.

What enables the teeth to do their job is the jaw. The jaw is structured so that the incisors can move independently while the rodent's cheeks are pulled in, allowing only certain materials to be ingested and hindering others from passing through. Rodents have been divided into three suborders according to jaw musculature: Sciuromorpha (squirrel-like rodents), Caviomorpha (cavylike rodents), and the largest suborder of rodents, Mymorpha (mouselike rodents). Those belonging to the latter suborder, namely mice and rats, have jaw muscles that enable them to gnaw through cement. If they can drill through cement, then imagine how easy and effortless it must be for them to make their way through your vegetable gardens, or through the deteriorating wood door leading to the basement.

Since mice are genetically similar to human beings, they are the most commonly used laboratory animals for medical research. While there are other mammals that are genetically similar to humans, using mice appears to be a more convenient and efficient means of experimentation. There are several reasons why medical experts have chosen to test procedures on mice and rats. Being small, they are easily handled when trained. Because they have short life spans and can reproduce quickly and in high volume, it is possible to follow the progress of a disease throughout an entire life cycle. Mice are used to test the safety of chemicals, household products, and pesticides that may be potentially harmful to humans. Mice also are used to determine the safety of drugs and vaccines. Standing in as substitutes for humans in biomedical research, mice—specifically the nude mouse, a hairless mutant discovered in the early 1960s—have been used to study cancer. Because the nude mouse is immunodeficient, it accepts tumor transplants from other species, enabling scientists to study tumor activity within an animal system. (University of California Center for Animal Alternatives)

Population Explosion

Not all rodents are prolific breeders. For instance, female mountain beavers breed for a short period during the spring and will bear only a couple of offspring at a time. On the other hand, mice mate up to seventeen times annually, with each litter containing four to nine offspring. The gestation period for female rodents is another factor contributing to the population explosion. It can take as little as sixteen days after conception—eighteen to twenty-one days for the common house mouse (*Mus musculus*)—for rodents to give birth to their litters.

High reproduction rates are only partly responsible for the high concentration of rodents in any given area. Another factor is the availability of food. If you feed them (intentionally or inadvertently), they will come. Where mice have access to food, you will find them in large numbers.

Not only will there be many of them, but they will be strong, healthy, and primed to reproduce.

Rodents are many things, but did you know that they also were *Guinness* record holders? A *Guinness Book of World Records* supplement to the December 5, 1998, edition of *The Mirror,* a London newspaper, called brown rats the "most prolific mammal," because scientists estimate that their population is about the same as that of humans—more than five billion. The beaver of North America received the title of "best builder" for their dam construction. Prairie dogs swept the "largest colony" category. In 1901, a series of prairie dog tunnels stretching about twenty-four thousand miles was discovered, and the number of inhabitants was roughly four hundred million.

2

Humans and Rodents

Some People Like Rodents

It might be difficult for many of you to comprehend, but there are some people who simply love rodents. Not just hamsters and guinea pigs, but mice and rats as well. There are newsletters, on-line news groups, and chat rooms dedicated to swapping information about beloved rodents and trading information on how to keep pet rats strong and healthy. So while you're masterminding ways to rid yourself of uninvited guests, some folks are figuring out the best ways to breed and feed them.

Selissa Leonard of Missouri currently owns approximately twenty rats and also breeds them. A self-professed animal lover, Leonard said her love of rats developed by default back in the days when she owned a pet python. The main course for pythons is rodents, and the cheapest and easiest method of feeding the python was breeding its food, Leonard says. But after a while she grew fond of the rats and chose them over the python, which she gave to her brother.

What is so endearing about rats? "They're really smart. You can teach them tricks. They are very affectionate, and they respond to their names," Leonard says. "And they're really easy to house-train." Leonard also mentioned that rats are "connoisseurs of fine food."

Those who are accustomed to rats are comfortable at Leonard's home, but most people find the setup "freaky," she says. "For some reason there's something about a rat's tail that drives people crazy. A lot of people are disturbed by the sight of it. Maybe it's because it has no fur."

But just because Leonard likes rats does not mean she is fond of all rodents. She says that in her experience she has found mice to be overly territorial and smelly. Rats, she says, are very clean and spend a substantial portion of the day grooming themselves, much like their enemies, cats.

Rodents on the Silver Screen

Mice and other rodents have found their way not only into your homes and gardens, but they have also invaded pop culture, making their presence known on the silver screen and television. The cartoon *Tom and Jerry*, created in the 1940s, follows the classic cat-and-mouse chase, with Jerry, the clever and cunning mouse, always victorious over his feline nemesis, Tom. Just as the dashing hero in film always gets the girl, Jerry always got his cheese, despite

Tom's efforts. One of the most important lessons learned from *Tom and Jerry* is that using your cat as a mouse catcher is not always the most effective method, which we will explore later. Predictably, each episode ended with Jerry outsmarting Tom, despite his best (and at times inventive) efforts to outwit the mouse. *Tom and Jerry* is really a cartoon satire of how mice outsmart people!

Another rodent that was portrayed as a force to be reckoned with was Mighty Mouse. With the creation of the Mighty Mouse character in 1955 came a new role for the species—mouse as hero. "Here I come to save the day" was his catchphrase—and save he did. Episode after episode, Mighty Mouse claimed victory over villains by using superpowers such as enhanced strength, the ability to fly, and again, mental prowess. This cartoon made the meek strong. It empowered kids (mice being the cartoon metaphor for smallness).

Then there is Mickey Mouse—one of the most beloved cartoon characters of all time. When Walt Disney introduced Mickey Mouse to the world of cartoon movies on November 12, 1928, in *Steamboat Willie,* parents were not impressed with his mischievous and disrespectful behavior. As time progressed, Mickey Mouse evolved into a charming, polite, demure, lovable character—a poster boy for all things good and innocent.

Not all rodents are portrayed as heroic do-gooders on the silver screen and television. In 1971 and 1972, Hollywood showed what happens when good rats go bad with the release of the horror film *Willard* and its sequel, *Ben*. In *Willard*, the title character is a loner who seeks revenge on his coworkers after his boss fires him from his job at his deceased father's company. But what sends Willard over the edge is the death of one of the rats that he has raised at home, which was killed at the office. To avenge the death of his rodent friend and the way he was treated in the office, he sends the remaining rats on a payback mission. Ben, who was one of Willard's rodent friends, comes back in the sequel to lead a pack of violent killer rats.

Rodents in Literature

Mice have also found a place in literature, specifically children's literature. In 1945, author E. B. White published his first children's book, *Stuart Little,* the title character and hero of which is a mouse.

Mrs. Frisby and the Rats of NIMH is yet another classic involving rats and mice. The tale, written by Robert C. O'Brien, revolves around a mouse named Mrs. Frisby who needs to move her family from a farm that is about to be overrun with plows and other dangerous machinery. She enlists the help of some rats who escaped from the National Institute of Mental Health. The book raises the key issue of the use of rats as part of medical experiments. Rodents also are portrayed in a positive light in other classics, such as the water rat in *The Wind in the Willows* by Kenneth Grahame, the dormouse in *Alice in Wonderland* by Lewis

Carroll, and in Beatrix Potter's stories *The Tale of Mrs. Tittlemouse* and *The Tale of Johnny Town-Mouse.*

The previously mentioned rodent celebrities are not in a league of their own, in fact they share the spotlight with numerous other rodents. The following rodents deserve an honorable mention:

Minnie Mouse, Mickey Mouse's sweetheart

"Three Blind Mice"

Rocky the Flying Squirrel, cartoon *Rocky and Bullwinkle*

Punxsutawney Phil, Groundhog Day (Feb. 2) forecaster

Templeton the Rat, *Charlotte's Web*

The mouse from "Androcles and the Lion," *Aesop's Fables*

Bernard and Bianca, *The Rescuers*

Rodents as Pets

When it comes to owning rodents as pets, mice and rats are not among the most popular. People usually prefer gerbils, hamsters, and guinea pigs. Another rodent that we have invited into our homes is the chinchilla. This batch of critters might be more successful than others in charming humans because they are considered "cuter" than mice or rats. There are other factors that make some rodents more practical pets than others. For instance, gerbils and guinea pigs are less likely to bite and are easier to handle than hamsters.

So over the course of history how did these pests become pets? Before chinchillas, hamsters, gerbils, and guinea pigs were allowed to live in domestic bliss, rats paved the way. Dating back to the Victorian period, people were breeding and selling rats as pets. Soon breeders started to get creative and bred fancy rats, which came in more colorful selections than the regular black, brown, or white ones. Currently there are nearly thirty varieties of fancy rats and numerous variations of fancy mice. Nowadays, nonfancy mice and rats are called feeder mice and feeder rats, which are bred specifically to feed to snakes. Bethesda Pet Shoppe in Maryland used to sell mice and rats, but it stopped when it realized that most of its customers purchased them to feed pet snakes.

In general, rodents have become popular pets because they are small, require very little maintenance, and their room and board is inexpensive. Although they have very sharp teeth, rodents that are accustomed to being held are unlikely to bite. For these reasons, many parents purchase rodents for their children. One key concern about pet rodents, especially mice and rats, is the chance that they carry diseases and illnesses. Selective breeding, or "fancying," has made the breeding of diseased rodents less likely, because fancy rodents have been bred in captivity in sterile environments.

Chinchillas

One of the few rodents regularly sold in pet stores is the chinchilla. One of the reasons they are considered choice pets is because people like to pet them. Because chinchillas are found in areas of high altitudes, such as the Andes, they have dense coats to help them survive frigid temperatures—each follicle can hold up to eighty hairs. Their plush fur has also been the cause of their demise. The Ancient Incans hunted them for their fur, and during the sixteenth century, Spanish explorers were transporting the fur back to Europe. The chinchilla fur trade industry continued to thrive, and chinchilla fur was in demand throughout the nineteenth century, until the species was nearly extinct. In the early 1920s, a mining engineer named M. F. Chapman gradually brought the chinchillas from the high altitudes to sea level to work on breeding them. It was not until the 1960s that the fur market died down and chinchillas became popular pets.

There are two species of chinchillas that belong to the family Chinchillidae. Unlike many other rodents, chinchillas have long life spans and can live up to twenty years. One of a chinchilla's most noticeable features are its ears, which are large and prominent. Another key characteristic of a chinchilla is the way it moves. Instead of scurrying like mice and rats, chinchillas tend to hop like rabbits. However, they are similar to rats in other ways. For instance, they handle food with their paws the same way rats do. They are also nocturnal creatures.

Chinchillas differ from other popular pet rodents in that they require additional care—and are much more expensive. It is imperative that chinchilla owners handle them with care to make sure they don't damage their coats. Part of the high maintenance regimen is a daily dust bath in volcanic ash or activated clay, which protects and conditions their coats.

Hamsters

Why do most people seem to prefer hamsters to gerbils? Because they think hamsters are cuter, according to Marcia Heintze of the Bethesda Pet Shoppe in Maryland. "It's more looks than anything else," Heintze says. Hamsters are small creatures, weighing in at around four ounces, and grow to only six or seven inches long. Unlike chinchillas, which have long life spans as far as rodents are concerned, the average life span of hamsters is around two and a half years.

Although experts say there are twenty-four hamster species, the golden hamster (*Mesocricetus auratus*) is the only one that has gained popularity as a pet. (The name can be misleading. As a result of breeding, there are

---

about twenty-five color variations of the golden hamster.) Again, what makes the hamster a convenient pet is its low maintenance. As long as it has food and water and a deep layer of bedding so it can burrow in its cage, the hamster will be content. But the golden hamster, also known as the Syrian hamster because that is where it originated, is not a social animal. They prefer to live independently, so housing a couple of hamsters in one cage is unwise, since they are also very aggressive with each other and cohabitation often ends in death for one or both. Heintze says that occasionally customers will return hamsters with the complaint that they bite. Since hamsters are nocturnal creatures that go into a deep sleep, if they are awoken suddenly, they tend to bite in response to being startled, so tread lightly.

According to Mark Sands of the Animal Hut in Washington, D.C., customers who are looking for mice or rats usually have owned a hamster in the past. This, he says, is because they all require the same care. So hamsters are the guinea pigs, so to speak, when it comes to determining if you want a pet mouse or rat.

Gerbils

Although gerbils are a popular pet rodent, they seem to have been dealt a bad hand in the reputation department. According to Sands, people dislike gerbils because they look like rats. But in comparison, the benefits of owning a gerbil far outweigh those associated with owning a hamster. For instance, gerbils are cleaner, more social, friendlier, less likely to bite, and are not as "smelly" as hamsters, says Marcia Heintze of the Bethesda Pet Shoppe. Gerbils are less susceptible to diseases, making them better pets than other rodents, such as mice, which contract and spread diseases easily. Also, they don't mind being held.

The Mongolian gerbil (*Meriones unguiculatus*) is the pet gerbil of choice, beating out thirteen others that belong to the genus. Keeping Mongolian gerbils as pets is a relatively new concept. Discovered in the 1860s, Mongolian gerbils did not become domesticated until scientists started to use them for research in the 1950s. Unlike hamsters, gerbils like to interact with their own kind. They tend to live in colonies and often employ the buddy system, but they do not socialize with outsiders. Contact with gerbils from another group is basically limited to females who mate with a male from another colony. The females then return to their original group to give birth and raise their litter, which contains about five offspring.

Gerbils are smaller than hamsters, weighing about three ounces and measuring about eight inches long, and live about two years longer, up to five years. One of the most important parts of their anatomy is the tail. The long furred tail—three to nine inches—is responsible for keeping the gerbil on its feet, providing it with balance while it's stationary or moving.

Wild gerbils and pet gerbils have different appetites and therefore different diets. Wild gerbils enjoy feasting on flowers, leaves, seeds, and insects, while pet gerbils prefer a vegetarian diet consisting of lettuce, carrots, and store-bought pet food. By nature, gerbils are burrowing creatures, so whether they are in a cage or out in the Sahara desert, during the day they can most likely be found under the ground, where they eat and sleep.

Guinea Pigs

The guinea pig claims the title of the most popular pet rodent. Today, we use the term "guinea pig" to describe situations in which something is being tried or tested for the

first time. The new meaning developed when guinea pigs were being used for pharmaceutical testing. But there is a much larger name game at work, as there are many theories on the origin of the term "guinea pig." Guinea pigs often making piglike grunts when they are touched might account for the "pig" part of the name. As for the "guinea" portion, people thought that guinea pigs originated in Guinea, when in fact they came from Guiana. Wild guinea pigs reside in high altitudes and grasslands in such places as Argentina, Brazil, Peru, and Uruguay.

Children might love these cuddly creatures because they are easily handled and generally well behaved, but they are not as popular among gardeners. To the dismay of those who raise gardens, guinea pigs love their veggies. Leafy green vegetables, carrots, peas, and dandelion leaves make up a healthy guinea pig's diet. They also like grass, flowers, clover, hay, and chickweed.

On average, guinea pigs measure eight inches long and live up to four years. Guinea pigs are no different from other domesticated rodents in that their coats come in a variety of colors (including black, brown, white, and occasionally red) and textures as a result of breeding. Different types include the Peruvian, satin, crested, Abyssinian, Alcapas, and the smooth-coated guinea pig.

A cautionary note to people purchasing guinea pigs for their children: guinea pigs cannot survive a drop. It is dangerous to leave a guinea pig on a high surface, such as a table, because they are not good at determining height and will plummet to their death.

3

What Is a Rodent?

Species

Rodents come in a variety of sizes and shapes, and you already know one of their key identifying characteristics: their unique dentition, or teeth. Unfortunately, scientists must use characteristics other than just teeth alone to determine how many species belong to the order Rodentia. Again, we can't deduce that it is a rodent merely because it is small, hairy, has whiskers and a long tail. It's not that easy. Insufficient fossil remains, the large number of different species, their small size, and the vast area over which they can be found contribute to the difficulty experts have run into when trying to discover new species. As the order grows, it becomes more challenging to determine where one species ends and a new one begins.

The order Rodentia is made up of three groups: sciuromorphs, myomorphs, and caviomorphs. These rodents are classified according to their jaw musculature. Sciuromorphs are squirrel-like rodents, which includes mountain beavers, pocket gophers, pocket mice, beavers, chipmunks, prairie dogs, springhares, and of course the many types of squirrels.

Mouselike rodents belong to the largest of the three suborders, Myomorpha. The suborder contains five families, the largest of which is the Muridae. This family contains some of the more familiar rodents, including mice, rats, gerbils, hamsters, and mole rats. This group's claim to fame is that its members have been able to survive and thrive on nearly every continent. The most notable survivor is the house mouse, which has overcome the frigid zone of South Georgia, an island near Antarctica.

The smallest suborder of rodents is the Caviomorpha. Most caviomorphs can be found in South America, including the largest rodent, the capybara, which weighs in at about 176 pounds and fifty-one inches long. Other caviomorphs are New and Old World porcupines, cavies, chinchilla rats, chinchillas, spiny rats, cane rats, African mole rats, and coypus.

Rats

Norway Rats

The Norway rat *(Rattus norvegicus)* was unintentionally introduced to North America by settlers arriving in ships from Europe in about 1775. Much to the chagrin of many Americans, they have now spread throughout all of the forty-eight contiguous states of the United States. Also called the brown rat, house rat, barn rat, sewer rat, wharf rat, or gray rat, Norway rats are usually reddish brown or reddish gray on top, and whitish gray on the belly. They have rather blunt muzzles and small, close-set eyes, and scaly, seminaked tails that are about as long as their head and body combined. And though the adult Norway rat is considered to be stocky and heavyset, on average one actually weighs only about one pound.

Unfortunately for us, Norway rats live in close association with people, though they do tend to be found at lower elevations as well. Like other rodents, they burrow to make nests under buildings, along stream banks, around ponds, and in garbage dumps and other suitable places. They usually line their nests with shredded paper, cloth, or other fibrous material. An interesting tip is that they tend to stick to the lower levels of multistory buildings, in spite of their ability to climb. So if you're looking to avoid the Norway rat, you might want to consider moving above the ground floor.

Since Norway rats are primarily nocturnal, they can also be avoided by staying away from infested areas during the evening hours. They usually become active at dusk, when they begin looking for food and water. This search is generally pretty simple for the rats, because they will eat any type of food, though they prefer cereal grains, meat and fish, nuts, and some types of fruit. Norway rats need at least one-half to one ounce of water daily if eating mostly dry foods, but less when moist foods are available. Be aware that the food items in our regular household garbage offer a fairly balanced diet for the rats and also satisfy their moisture needs.

And don't think you're safe from meeting a Norway rat just because it is still daylight. Some may be active during the day if the rat population is high, if they are disturbed by a change in the weather or some local construction, or if their food source is threatened. A Norway rat will travel three hundred feet or more every day just to obtain food and water, though the territories of most rats span a 50- to 150-foot radius of the nest.

You might be tempted to think you have an advantage over these rodents, who have poor eyesight beyond three or four feet, but their other senses have adapted to make up for this shortcoming. Despite the fact that, on top of weak eyesight, Norway rats are also essentially color-blind, they are able to detect motion up to thirty to fifty feet away. They do so by relying more on their hearing and superior senses of smell, taste, and touch. The frequency range of their hearing is fifty kilohertz, compared to the twenty kilohertz frequency of humans. This means that they can use hearing to locate objects within a few inches. And they use their olfactory senses to recognize the odors of pathways, members of the opposite sex who might want to mate, and to differentiate not only between members of their own colonies and strangers, but also between weak and strong rats. An excellent sense of taste allows Norway rats to detect contaminants in their food at levels as low as .5 parts per million, which could lead to the rejection of baited food containing poison. Sensitive body hairs and whiskers help them explore their surroundings, and they prefer to keep a stationary object on at least one side of them as they are traveling. This explains why they commonly move along walls, making walls a bad place for you to be standing around at night in any infested area. So watch your step!

The rapid life cycle of the Norway rat helps keep the population up. Living only an average of a thousand days, the maximum life span would be about two thousand days. Two months after the rats are born they are mature, and in twenty-two to twenty-four days after that, females are usually ready to give birth. A Norway rat usually breeds twelve times in one year, producing two to twenty-two young each time. The newborn rats can eat solid food at two and a half to three weeks and become completely independent at about three to four weeks. Until then, they are given milk and are bathed by the adults. But don't think that the mother is sitting idle during that time. Female Norway rats have been known to mate within a day after a litter is born!

If you not only want to defensively avoid the Norway rat but are also looking to offensively eradicate them, remember that glue boards will be ineffective on large rodents, and that snap traps and live traps will work better. The most effective method for the Norway rat may be the use of weather-proof bait blocks. (Much more on traps will be provided in chapter 5.)

All rats, regardless of their specific species, share one characteristic: neophobia, or fear of new objects. This makes these creatures wary of and sensitive to any change in their environment. This trait makes outwitting rats more complex. As you will find out later, there are ways in which you can get around this and even use it to your advantage.

Roof Rats

Roof rats, ship rats, black rats, and fruit rats are all various names for *Rattus rattus.* The roof rat is smaller and more slender than the Norway rat, weighing in at six to twelve ounces. A baby roof rat most likely will grow to be around six to eight inches long. Where it makes up for its smaller size is in the length of its tail, which can reach up to ten inches in length. Roof rats originated in Asia but are commonly found in southern coastal states in the United States near water. But that doesn't mean that if you live inland in the Northeast you won't see a roof rat. They like to live in elevated areas, so you most likely will find them living in trees, attics, or on the tops of buildings and homes. Don't keep your head in the clouds, however, because they sometimes burrow under foliage or in basements and sewers.

Roof rats are usually a brownish black or gray and have a black or gray underbelly. There are a few characteristics that, if you get really close to them, will help you determine if you've come in contact with a roof rat. You would only know this by touching it, but the roof rat's fur is smooth and soft. Its eyes are very large, and its ears appear to be almost furless. The tail is dark and scaly and is longer than the entire length of the rat's body. These characteristics can help you determine if you have a Norway rat or a roof rat because Norway rats have small, beady eyes, small, furry ears, and their tails are shorter than the length of their bodies.

Female roof rats have four to six litters per year, with six to eight offspring per litter. As young roof rats mature they develop keen senses of hearing, smell, touch, and taste, but they have poor vision and are color-blind. As you know, rats will eat just about anything you put in front of them, but even rats have their favorites. The roof rat prefers to nibble on veggies, fruits, eggs, seeds, and occasionally, cereals. They must drink an ounce of water and eat about an ounce of food daily to survive.

Mice

Dormice

During the winter months in northern areas of the world, some dormice curl themselves up into little balls and hibernate. Dormice, such as the common dormouse, *Mus-*

cardinus arvellanarius, are usually found in grassy woodlands, where they will hibernate in the abundant trees. During the spring and summer months they make a special point to eat large quantities of insects in preparation for hibernation. They also like flowers, pollen, seeds, hazelnuts, blackberries, raspberries, and various other nuts and fruits.

While their name suggests that they resemble a mouse, dormice are more similar in appearance to squirrels. Generally, their tails are bushy and longer than that of the average mouse. The size of a dormous varies from species to species but can measure anywhere from seven to twenty centimeters. The size of the tail ranges from six to twenty centimeters. The common dormouse weighs about three-quarters of an ounce before hibernation, and puts on an additional one-quarter ounce during hibernation. The fur of the common dormouse is a golden brown, but colors vary. These nocturnal creatures have a white underbelly and throat.

You can consider the dormouse a well-traveled and cultured rodent, as they can be found all over the world, including Israel, Bulgaria, Africa, Turkey, and in isolated areas of North and South America, to name a few. The dormouse's tiny clawed feet, which make it easy to grip branches tightly, make it suitable for life in the woodlands. Unlike other rodents, like the roof rat, the dormouse has sharp eyesight, which comes in handy as they make their way from tree to tree.

Female dormice do not produce many litters annually. Some, like the garden dormouse, only breed once a year, and the common dormouse breeds maybe three times annually, producing three to nine offspring.

House Mice

The house mouse, *Mus musculus,* is one of the most well-known rodents. You might know this mouse as the domestic house mouse or common house mouse. Because they are small, quick, and nocturnal, it is easy for them to go unnoticed for long periods of time, which gives them more time to do their damage. One of the factors that works to their advantage (not to ours) is that house mice are prolific breeders who, after they are born, reach sexual maturity in a little over a month. The gestation period for females is about nineteen days, and they breed about eight times a year, averaging about six offspring per litter. If you do the math, that means one female can give birth to over forty baby house mice a year. While life expectancy is about one year, mice have lived to be five and six years old.

Like roof rats, house mice have keen senses of smell, touch, taste, and hearing, but they have difficulty seeing past six inches in front of them, and they are color-blind. Their diminished eyesight does not stop them from being excellent climbers, who can run up textured walls, or good jumpers. Basically they are the supermen of rodents, leaping twelve inches into the air, jumping eight feet from a surface without sustaining any injury, running along pipes and wires while maintaining perfect balance. Mice prefer to nest in areas that are dark and abandoned. They also like to live in areas where they have access to nesting materials, such as cotton, fabrics, wall insulation, and cotton. As for their personalities, mice are very social, curious creatures that like to explore new places, including your home. Their curious nature sometimes makes it difficult to establish a pattern because they tend to change their routes.

These mice are tiny, with a combined head and body length reaching four inches on the larger side, a tail that is just over two inches, and weighing just about an ounce on the heavy side. Fur color ranges from various shades of gray to light brown, with an off-white or light gray belly. They have small eyes, large ears with a small amount of fur on them, and a scaly, nearly naked tail.

Mice are not big eaters and tend to consume small amounts of food at one sitting. They eat insects, seeds, and grain, but that does not mean they won't eat any of your other foods. Some of their favorite foods are meat, bread, bacon, grains, cereal, oatmeal, peanut butter, and cheese. Mice can go for several days without drinking water because they get their supply of water from food. You can catch them eating during two main periods of the day: at dusk and right before dawn. Of course, they still snack in between.

Pocket Mice

Pocket mice get their un- usual name not from their size but because of the way they carry food in the pouches of their cheeks. These small jumping rodents (of the family *Heteromyi- dae*) can be found in North America, South America, Canada, and parts of Mexico. What makes it difficult to iden- tify a pocket mouse, if you're not familiar with them, is the fact that there are several different species that differ greatly in appearance. They can vary in length from three to twelve inches from species to species. But they all have powerful hind legs and feet that enable them to jump with precision or provide steady support. Although most pocket mice live in burrows mainly in deserts or desertlike areas, there is one species, *heteromys,* that prefers to reside in balmy woodlands.

Kangaroo mice of the species *microdipodops* can be found in the western region of the United States. Their front legs are short, but their hind legs are one of the most important features. The name implies that they move like kangaroos, hopping around from place to place, and rightly so. Their strong, elongated hind legs enable them to balance and hop solely on their hind legs. They also have long tails that help them keep their equilibrium. Since these mice live mainly in desert areas, their feet come equipped with stiff hairs that enable them to hop across areas without sinking into sandy surfaces.

As with all rodents, breeding success is directly related to the availability of food. Under good conditions and with abundant food sources, females can give birth to litters of eight offspring three times a year. Like house mice, the gestation period for pocket mice is about a month. Life expectancy is about one year, but there are a few known cases of pocket mice that lived up to four years.

Deer Mice

Deer mice, *Peromyscus maniculatus,* inhabit a wide variety of regions, including Canada, the United States, and Mexico. The adult deer mouse is tan or brown (young deer mice are gray) with round ears and white underparts, which is why they are often called white-footed mice. The total length of the deer mouse, including its tail, can range from six to eight inches. The bicolored tail is quite long, accounting for about half of its body length. The deer mouse tends to keep to itself because it is often preyed upon. They tuck themselves away in nests that are usually located inside trees, under structures, or in abandoned squirrel nests in heavily forested areas. In an attempt to make themselves as comfortable as possible, they use tree bark and leaves to line their nests. Although they have been known to venture into homes and other buildings when winter comes, they are not half as destructive as house mice and other rodents such as the Norway rat. For the most part, deer mice are just happy living in the forest, nibbling on fruits, trying to avoid danger.

On a negative note, deer mice have been associated with spreading deadly hantaviruses that cause hantavirus pulmonary syndrome (HPS) in humans. This disease will be discussed at greater length in chapter 4, but it is important to note that people are exposed to the disease when they come in contact with droppings from an infected rodent, which can be found in burrows, homes, garages, and various other areas frequented by deer mice.

> Deer mice communicate with one another by drumming their hind feet on the ground. It was suspected that rodents developed this behavior as a means of alerting others of impending danger, but many speculate that it's a way to show excitement.

Gray Squirrel

If you're wondering whether or not the gray squirrel is gray, the answer is no. Its fur is a combination of gray, brown, and yellow on top, and white and gray on the underbelly. The long, soft, bushy tail, which is about eight to ten inches long, is silver and white. The tail is a source of warmth and provides balance, which they need when they are scaling trees and landing on bird feeders. Squirrels also use their tails to communicate with one another. The gray squirrel, *Sciurus carolinensis,* is about sixteen to twenty inches long and can weigh up to twenty-five ounces. Gray squirrels produce two litters a year and live for one year on average. Domesticated squirrels can live up to twelve years, which can mean only one thing: life on the streets is tough.

There are many species of squirrels, which are usually classified into two groups: tree-dwelling squirrels and ground squirrels. Gray squirrels are tree dwellers, which mean that they pose a serious threat to your nut trees and bird feeders. Gray squirrels prefer beech and oak trees because they can dine on their nuts. In addition to exploiting nut trees and bird feeders, they also indulge in fruit, flowers, seeds, insects, bird eggs, peanut butter, apples, plant buds, and mushrooms. Baby birds are also part of their diets, which is no surprise, since gray squirrels are omnivorous.

Gray squirrels can be found in several areas of the United States, but if you reside in the eastern United States, then you've most definitely been exposed to them. Areas heavy in vegetation, like parks and forests, are some of their favorites. Gray squirrels are forward-thinking creatures, so they bury nuts during fall with the intention of going back to them later during the winter.

Gray squirrels are known for stripping bark off of hardwood trees. As a result of this pastime, they are commonly referred to as "tree rats." Gnawing and stripping a tree of its bark can kill the tree or make it susceptible to certain diseases.

Red Squirrel

Red squirrels, *Tamiascuirus hudsonicus,* are more petite than gray squirrels, weighing in at nine ounces on the high end. Their diets do not differ from that of gray squirrels, except that in addition to seeds, fruits, berries, mushrooms, and nuts, red squirrels like fungi. Red squirrels are especially fond of pinecones. They are very quick creatures and often can be found darting around. During the fall, they zip about, collecting seeds and nuts for winter, and during the winter they run about furiously looking for buried munitions. The red squirrel is more compulsive about having food in reserve than the gray squirrel. Even if they have plenty of food buried in a given area, they are constantly searching for more food.

These squirrels are found in North America. Red squirrels produce litters twice a year, with litters averaging five offspring. Their coats are usually a brownish red with a white or off-white underbelly. Their black eyes are encircled by a white ring.

Muskrats

As you might have guessed, muskrats *(Ondatra zibethicus)* have a musky odor, hence the fitting moniker. But they emit the strong odor for a practical reason: to mark their territory. Muskrats are grouped with voles and lemmings in the subfamily Microtinae, which for the most part embodies one main characteristic: a passion for burrowing. The gestation period for females is twenty-five to thirty days, and they produce six litters a year. Because they can reproduce quickly, muskrat populations are usually on the high side despite natural disasters and disease. They also have many enemies, such as foxes, coyotes, and raccoons, who prey on young muskrats. On average, muskrats grow to be about twenty inches in length, but there are cases where they grow thirty inches long. The average life span is two to three years. Muskrats are various shades of brown, ranging from light brown to an almost black shade of brown. Their tails are rudderlike, which helps them navigate in the water. Their front feet, as opposed to their webbed rear feet, are small, making them well equipped for digging and holding on to objects.

Muskrats are aquatic creatures. They will set up residence anyplace where water accumulates, even a ditch. Although they are mainly vegetarians and can wipe out nearby vegetation if given a chance, they will eat frogs, fish, and other seafood.

Although they enjoy being in and near water, that doesn't stop them from traveling into your garden or seeking vegetation that happens to be in your backyard. Being nocturnal creatures, they do their damage at night, so only when you wake up do you see their handiwork.

Beavers

The way that beavers are characteristically portrayed as having prominent front teeth makes it undeniable that beavers, *Castor canadensis,* are rodents. But what sets them apart from other rodents is the bright, shockingly orange color of their teeth. Beavers are also on the larger side, weighing up to sixty pounds and registering in at about four feet in length. In fact, they are the largest rodent in North America.

You would never know it just by looking at them, but these stocky creatures love to swim. Beavers use their front paws to comb their waterproof fur and carry objects. The webbed back paws are used for swimming. The flat paddle-shaped tail is covered with waterproof oil and is used as a navigational tool to steer the beaver around. To warn other beavers of impending danger, a beaver will smack its tail against the water.

Beavers live near the water, on or in the banks along a river or lake in more northern areas of the United States. Each family of beavers constructs its own permanent dwelling—their lodge. To protect themselves from their enemies, which include trappers, wolverines, lynxes, and wolves, beavers build at least two entrances to their lodges beneath the water. A beaver can remain underwater for up to fifteen minutes.

Beavers are most active during a twelve-hour period from the late afternoon until the early morning, which means this is the time when they will be doing most of their damage. After arriving in Canada, early Europeans realized that the huge beaver population was quite valuable, which gave birth to the fur-trading industry that almost decimated the number of beavers in Canada and the northern United States. Today, however, the beaver population has rebounded and continues to prosper.

Beavers eat berries and fruit. But the pièce de résistance is tree bark. They consider it a favorite pastime. Like many rodents, beavers do most of their gnawing at night.

So while you are having pleasant dreams, beavers are gnawing away on area trees and, in many cases, chopping them down. Beavers have been known to cut down several trees in one evening. And they don't just target any trees; it seems as though they have an appreciation for beauty and often target the most attractive trees in the area, such as cherry trees, birch, and pine.

Beavers also expend their energies building dams. These dams protect the nearby wooded areas from flooding, but they sometimes cause flooding by holding back too much water. Once beavers target a shallow area of water, they gnaw down a number of trees. They then drag these logs into the water and continue to add mud and twigs as necessary. After they've created the dam and its subsequent calm pool, they build their lodges on or near this miniature pond. If the beavers sense that they won't be able to drag the logs, they build a canal. This allows them to float the log to the desired spot.

Each spring, female beavers give birth to between two and eight offspring. These litters, which are also called kits, usually average four babies. Females begin breeding after the age of two. Beavers mate for life and remain together to raise their family. They are communal creatures that enjoy spending time with one another in groups called colonies. If local food supplies are abundant, then colonies can reach up to twelve to fifteen individuals. If food is in demand and there is little of it, then younger ones will be forced to fend for themselves. While it takes a whole village of beavers to cause mass destruction, it can take only a few to make your life miserable. Fortunately, humans get a little reprieve during the winter, which is when beavers hibernate. As for the fall, they spend most of that season gathering food in preparation for winter.

The beaver was named the Canadian national emblem in 1975. The beaver signifies Canadian independence from the royal crown.

Voles

There are several species of vole, which differ according to habitat, coloring, and size. Most voles are classified under the genus *Microtus*. There are the prairie voles, meadow voles, long-tailed voles, pine or woodland voles, montane voles, Mexican voles, water voles, and red-back voles to name a few. Some of the names indicate which environments the particular species tend to populate. Prairie voles can be found in grasslands, marshlands, and prairies. Meadow voles are more at home in wet meadows, while pine voles like to call pine forests and orchards home. As the name suggests, water voles can be found living near water, setting up shop in stream banks and lakeshores. But for the most part, voles share several distinct characteristics, such as their small rotund shape and their short legs and tails. Like the rest of their bodies, their eyes are small, and their ears are almost hidden. Their fur is thick and is usually brown or gray, although there are several possible color variations. Voles range in size anywhere from five to ten inches long, depending on the species. Females have one to five litters annually, giving birth to three to six young each time.

Voles are known to cause damage to forests and field crops, such as grains and potatoes. Voles girdle trees, which means they gnaw at and eat bark around the circumference of a tree, eventually killing it. Not only are crops eaten and completely destroyed by voles, but the runways that they use also tend to disrupt crop irrigation by rerouting existing water systems. Their burrows also ruin lawns, golf courses, and cause an array of landscaping problems. Some voles, such as the pine vole, prefer to burrow and use a complex underground tunnel system, instead of the above-ground runways used by long-tailed voles. Fortunately, voles don't pose as much of a health risk as some other rodents, but that doesn't mean you shouldn't be careful. They have been known to carry some diseases, such as plague and tularemia.

Lemmings

Lemmings *(Lemmus lemmus)* are found in most northern parts of North America, British Columbia, and various areas between Scandinavia and Siberia. Since they are vegetarians, humans have to pay special attention to their gardens and foliage in the area. Like voles, they live in underground burrows in which they nest. Lemmings are four to seven inches long, including their short tails. Their soft fur usually is auburn or a shade of gray, with a lighter underbelly. They have short legs and small ears. The gestation period is around twenty days, after which up to nine offspring can be born.

Porcupines

One of the largest rodents in North America is the tree porcupine (*Erethizon dorsatum*), which can weigh up to and over twenty pounds. But the feature they are most known for is their quill-covered body. With the exception of the face, underbelly, and tail, their bodies are covered with these rigid spines. Their quills enable them to challenge

their enemies, as they know that if the situation becomes too hairy and their enemy moves to attack, their quills will stop them in their tracks.

Unlike most of the rodents we've taken a look at, female porcupines give birth to one litter in the spring annually, which usually produces only one offspring. Their gestation period is also uncharacteristically long for a rodent: seven months. As suggested by their name, tree porcupines enjoy eating trees. But not just any trees. They do have a few favorites, including spruce, elm, and hemlock. If you have anything made of wood in your yard, and porcupines are in the area, you are at great risk of having materials, tools, and furniture destroyed. They also like to feed on rosebushes, pansies, and various crops in vegetable and fruit gardens.

Chipmunks

If you take a quick glance at a chipmunk (family *Tamias*), you will probably mistake one for a baby squirrel, as they look very similar. They are usually tan with white and dark stripes down their backs. And like squirrels, chipmunks love to nibble on seeds and nuts. They range in size from three to eight inches in length and weigh up to five ounces. You probably have noticed that many of the names of these rodents are directly linked to one of their identifying characteristics, i.e., the muskrat was named so for the strong odor it emits. The same rule can be applied to the name of the chipmunk. Chipmunks can be very vocal at times, and it is nearly impossible to ignore the unique noise they make, which sounds like a "chip." Chipmunks usually make this noise to notify others of impending danger. They also seem to have a chipper countenance and are known for the abrupt manner at which they dart around. Unfortunately, these chipper critters don't dart past your nut and fruit trees without cleaning them out first. If it were up to rodents like chipmunks and squirrels, you would not have one walnut to harvest when the season was over. This is because they prepare for the barren winter months by pillaging your yard. But the most damage occurs when chipmunks make a run for your flower beds. Garden bulbs are at risk of being eaten by chipmunks, so keep a close eye on your flowers if you know that chipmunks are in the area.

Prairie Dogs

The prairie dog, *Cynomys ludovicianus*, craves companionship. They are very social creatures and thrive on communal living in prairie dog towns. These towns are made up of intricate underground tunnel systems broken down into smaller units called wards, which are then broken down into even smaller units called coteries, which in turn are broken down into family units. The largest town, found in Texas, was 100 miles wide, 250 miles long.

These creatures are about fifteen to eighteen inches long and weigh about three pounds. The black-tailed prairie dog is tan with white underparts and a black-topped tail. The short legs contrast sharply with their large feet and talonlike claws. They produce one litter a year with up to six offspring. Prairie dogs eat grass, insects, and available vegetation. Since they do not store food in their burrows, prairie dogs look for their food when they are hungry and eat it fresh. Since their communities are so large, their eating habits can wipe out vegetation in entire areas. What is not eaten entirely is left destroyed by partial gnawing.

In addition to farmers, hawks, foxes, and eagles are also on the list of prairie dog predators. The mounds that lead to the entrance of their burrows help prairie dogs keep watch for impending danger. They alert others in the town by chirping. With eleven identified distinguishable calls and a series of postures, prairie dogs are considered excellent communicators.

Gophers

Gophers—also known as pocket gophers—are best known for their expert digging abilities and their external cheek pouches, which they use to carry food and other materials. What makes them such successful diggers and burrowers are their clawed front paws, their sensitive whiskers, which help them navigate tunnel systems in the dark, their short, thin hair, and powerful upper bodies. It also helps that they can use their teeth to dig through soil while their lips close tightly behind incisor teeth, keeping dirt out of their mouths.

Pocket gophers can reach up to fifteen inches in length. They range in color from shades of dark brown to cream with fine fur. Gophers have a life expectancy of three years, produce up to three litters a year, each litter averaging six offspring.

Being vegetarians, pocket gophers like to eat trees, grass, shrubs, and various other plants. Occasionally, they venture about twelve inches from the opening of their burrow and eat above ground, but for the most part, they dine below, eating the roots of plants or pulling the entire plant down into the burrow. Unlike prairie dogs, gophers are not social creatures. They keep to themselves and plow through their burrows solo.

The best way to determine if you have a gopher on the premises is to identify a mound. The loosened dirt formed by the action of the gopher digging underneath forms the mound, and if the soil is fresh then you probably have a gopher problem. The mounds are usually U-shaped with a plugged-off hole to one side of them.

Marmots

There are currently fourteen recognized species of marmots, which are large rodents with yellowish-brown or brown fur, usually about the size of a housecat. The head and body average about sixteen to twenty inches, not including a tail of about four to seven inches. Generally, marmots weigh about five to ten pounds and are considered to be fairly heavy-bodied rodents. Mating takes place in March or April, followed by a gestation period of thirty-one to thirty-two days. Traditionally, these rodents give birth to only one litter a year. Young are born blind and reach their own sexual maturity after twelve months. The average total lifespan is four to five years.

Marmots live mostly in open woods or rocky ravines and tend to search for food and move about during the day. They can be found in North America and Eurasia. They enjoy feasting on tender plants for the majority of their diet. At the end of the day they return home to the dens in their extensive burrows, which may have multiple entrances and may run four to five feet deep and twenty-five to thirty feet long. These dens provide the necessary shelter for the hibernation period, from October to February. After this winter sleep the marmot will come out of his ground "to see his shadow," as we humans like to call it. That's right. Groundhog Day, the only United States holiday named after an animal, is inspired by a marmot—the groundhog.

But just because the marmot is celebrated with its own day (albeit misnamed) in the United States, it doesn't mean that it is as revered in other countries. In fact, in some parts of the world, marmot meat is quite the delicacy, and their fur is considered to be a great prize. And in agricultural areas, certain types of marmots are detested for doing substantial damage to local crops.

Weird Rodents That Would Be Scary to Have Anywhere Near Your Home

Capybaras

The capybara is the largest rodent alive, which is reason enough for most people to fear it. With an average body length of forty-two to fifty-three inches, a shoulder height of twenty to twenty-four inches, a male's weight varying from 77 to 140 pounds, and a female's weight varying from 80 to 145 pounds, one capy-bara could easily intimidate any human. But don't expect to run into one unless you live in South or Central America, where capybaras live in large groups along the banks of rivers and lakes. They usually enjoy resting on land in the sunshine, but if they sense any danger, they will dive into the water for cover. In fact, the capybara spends so much time in or near the water that during the sixteenth century it was declared by the Vatican to be a fish, which allowed it to be eaten during Lent!

Looking much like an overgrown guinea pig, their nos-trils and their small eyes are set toward the top of the head, and they have a large bump in the middle of the top of their nose, which is thought to be a scent gland, possibly used for marking territory. Their front legs are shorter than their rear legs, and their skin is tough and covered with thin hair usually ranging in color from brown to red. A capybara's toes are webbed, with four toes on the front feet and three toes on the rear. Being herbivores, they en-joy eating grasses and other aquatic vegetation.

A group of capybaras usually includes a dominant male and several females, along with subordinate males and young. Communication is through a series of clicks, grunts, and whistles, along with scent from glandular se-cretions. In the wild, the natural life span is eight to ten years, but that number drops to four when they are hunted. Though not considered endangered, they are protected in some areas because of overhunting. Natural predators include jaguars and caimans. In the zoo, capybaras can live to be over twelve years old.

Capybaras mate in the water just before the rainy season begins, and females give birth on land usually 100 to 110 days later, though gestation can be as long as 150 days. Each annual litter consists of two to eight young. All females care for and nurse their young, which are weaned in about sixteen weeks. Sexual maturity is reached at eighteen months.

Just knowing that the capybara is the largest rodent alive would be enough to make most people cringe. But don't be so quick to judge. Though capybaras are admittedly huge for rodents, they are surprisingly docile and friendly! Their gregarious good humor makes them both likable and gentle.

Jirds

Jirds are relatives of the gerbil family. They look similar to gerbils, only a bit larger (an adult weighs one to three ounces). Most people don't really know what a jird is, let alone that there is more than one kind. Types range from Shaw's jirds, to Libyan to Sundevall's to Persian. In short, a jird is not just a jird is not just a jird. What's more is that though they may seem like "weird rodents" to some, they are increasingly being kept as pets!

For the most part, all jirds are fairly similar, despite some exceptions. The Shaw's jird's natural habitat is coastal desert areas, which can be found in North Africa and the Middle East. Sundevall's jirds tend to live in a wide range of dry habitats from Morocco to Pakistan. Persian jirds come from many parts of central Asia, including Turkey, Iran, Afghanistan, and many parts of ex-Soviet central Asia such as Turkmenistan and Azerbaijan. Most jirds enjoy regions that are flat and somewhat desertlike. Shaw's jirds generally live in tunnels excavated in deep clay, adding chambers for food storage and breeding. Those of the Persian variety often simply shelter under overhanging rocks. The burrows that they do dig are fairly simple and have few entrances and few chambers. Furthermore, Persian jirds will take advantage of human habitation, often living under walls, on the banks of irrigation ditches, and in the ruins of buildings.

Libyan jirds and Shaw's jirds are almost identical in size and appearance, though the Libyan's attractiveness as a pet is diminished by its shy demeanor and reluctance to breed in captivity. The Perisian jird is larger than the Shaw's jird, about six inches in length and with a tail that is about 15 percent longer than the body.

In the wild, their diet mainly consists of dry plant material and cereals, but they do enjoy fresh vegetables when available. Jird communication is not very vocal; they mostly use a system of thumping with the hind feet, much like the Mongolian gerbil. On the whole, they have a life span of about five to seven years, and a gestation period of twenty-four to twenty-six days. Most jirds are active during both day and night, though they are often thought to be primarily nocturnal. Amazingly, in the wild, a male jird may mate up to two hundred times in a single day!

Hutias

Hutias are broad-headed, robust ratlike rodents of the family Capromyidae with small eyes and ears and coarse, yellowish to reddish brown or black fur. Averaging eight to twenty-four inches in length without their tail, they are most commonly found in the forests of the Antilles and northern Venezuela. Hutias are primarily vegetarian, eating a diet of leaves, bark, and fruit, with the occasional lizard or other small animal thrown in. They are mostly nocturnal, though that depends on whether they are Cuban, Jamaican, Bahaman, or Hispaniolan hutias. Also, those like the dwarf hutia live on dry islets, while others like the Cabrera's hutia are mainly arboreal, building their nests in trees.

Unfortunately, hutias are becoming scarce in several areas. Two genera and several species are now extinct, with the bushy-tailed hutia and dwarf hutia well on their way. This decline is most likely the result of destruction of habitat, natural predators like the mongoose, and not-so-natural predators like man, hunting hutias for food and sport.

Flying Squirrels

Flying squirrels are not true members of the squirrel family. They don't even really fly. So what *is* true about this most enigmatic little rodent? Their body length is usually about eight inches, half of which is taken up by a flat beaverlike tail that curls up to resemble the tail of a squirrel only when the animal is up and active. This tail is used for steering when the squirrels are gliding through the air.

Yes, the flying squirrel does glide through the air. They have folds of skin between their legs that they stretch out to act like a parachute as they glide from tree to tree. The average flying squirrel can travel about three feet horizontally for every one foot it falls when gliding, and it is even able to change direction and speed or slow down through the use of those special folds of skin. They can be found in North America, Central America, and the Old World.

Flying squirrels are nocturnal and can actually be quite noisy at night as they run about chirping and whistling, grinding their teeth, and gnawing on nuts. In fact, this nightly noise might be the most pesky part about these animals. People who keep flying squirrels as pets have noted the nocturnal noises but are usually quick to say that they never keep them awake. And there are other benefits to keeping a flying squirrel as a pet. They generally don't harbor fleas, lice, ticks, mites, or any other parasites that might transmit disease.

Flying squirrels enjoy a diet of seeds, nuts, insects, fruits, and vegetables. They might even eat birds' eggs or catch and eat other rodents. Calcium is also an important part of their diet because flying squirrels have very light fragile bones for gliding, and without enough calcium they will develop deficiencies that will kill them. This deficiency is one reason why wild flying squirrels live only a few years, as opposed to the ten- to fifteen-year life span of those in captivity.

Sexual maturity is reached at the age of about one year. The gestation period for a pregnant flying squirrel is usually about forty days, and she will normally give birth to two to four babies, but under good environmental conditions she may give birth to up to seven!

Maras

The mara is a South American rodent that lives in harsh conditions near dried-out riverbeds and in thorny scrub in the arid and rocky expanses and grasslands of Argentina and Patagonia. They grow much taller than the average rodent, reaching almost two feet tall when standing, and weigh between fifteen and twenty pounds when fully grown. The mara's head and body are brown, the belly is white, and the rump is almost black, with a prominent white fringe around the base. Interestingly, they are quite rabbitlike in their habits and even actually resemble local versions of hares. With the body of a rabbit, except for slightly smaller ears and longer legs, the mara walk, run, or gallop along. Sometimes they even hop with a gait that closely resembles that of a hare, though it is admittedly a bit more like that of a kangaroo at times. Maras have been spotted running at nearly thirty miles per hour for a distance of over half a mile!

In captivity, maras are fed a diet of rabbit pellets, grass, clover, fruits, and vegetables. When living in the wild, they are grazing animals and live in communal burrows that they dig themselves or find abandoned by other animals. They often inhabit these homes for three or more years. The community may include upward of fifty maras; despite such a large crowd, the animals manage to maintain their monogamy and remain bonded to one partner for life. Maras communicate with one another by emitting a low grumble that can be heard only a few meters away from the rodent making it.

Under bushes, adult female maras will normally burrow and give birth at one time to a maximum of three young. More often than not, they give birth to two at a time. For several weeks after the birth, the mother and her babies will remain in the burrow together.

Coypus

Coypus, also known as nutrias, are South American rodents with reddish brown or yellowish brown outercoats of coarse guard hairs, dark gray soft undercoats, webbed hind feet, and very, very strong orange incisors. They are robust and muskratlike, with small eyes and ears. Long scaly tails are included in a body length that varies from seventeen to twenty-five inches, and usually weighs about seventeen and a half pounds. As semiaquatic animals, copyus live in burrows in swampy areas, subsisting mainly on freshwater plants. Adults produce litters of two to eight young per year, with a gestation period of about 135 days.

Unfortunately for coypus, their fur is valuable. The soft undercoat is often processed by furriers to resemble the beaver's pelt. Persistent hunting in the nineteenth and early twentieth centuries led to a decline in population. As a result, in an effort to increase breeding, the coypu was introduced into North America and Europe. In particular, the rodent was introduced into the United States from Argentina

in 1937 as an addition to the collection of the Avery Island
nature preserve on the southern fringes of Louisiana. When
a hurricane resulted in their release into the surrounding
marshes, the rodents spread rampantly across the southern
region of the state. Within five years, coypus were causing
the rampant decline of the native muskrat.

What does a state do in such a situation? The Louisiana
Nature Center held a Nutria Festival in 1993 and 1994, featuring the theme "If you can't beat 'em, eat 'em." Recipes
for coypus were created just for the occasion, and local
chefs prepared the dishes. That's one mighty interesting
way to outwit rodents.

Pacaranas

Pacaranas, also known as Branick's rats, are endangered
South American rodents native to the valleys and eastern
lower slopes of the Andes Mountains. They are heavy-
bodied with small ears, a relatively large head, and coarse,
white-spotted black or brown fur. Their features also include rounded snouts speckled with long whiskers. Small
ears and short legs with long, sharp claws on their feet
complete the illustration of the average Pacarana. Overall
they resemble guinea pigs.

As rodents go, pacaranas are fairly large, averaging
thirty-five to thirty-nine inches in length, including their
thick and hairy tail, and they usually grow to weigh in at
about thirty-three pounds. In fact, the only living rodent

larger than the pacarana is the capybara and the beaver. Pacaranas eat a diet consisting mainly of leaves, fruit, and other vegetation, such as stems. As for their dwellings, they take shelter in rock piles, crevices, or underground burrows. But don't be surprised to hear that they have also been known to sleep in trees, since they seem to be more suited to climbing branches than to walking along solid ground. Also of note is that the gestation period for pacaranas is similar to that of humans, about nine months, which is unusually long for a rodent. Females usually give birth to one or two young at a time.

Pacaranas have what scientists consider to be highly developed social behaviors because they use a number of different growls, hisses, and whimpers to communicate with one another. The same studies that provided information about their social behaviors also often revealed that the rodent is highly amicable and good-natured. But unfortunately we waited until they were already endangered before we made efforts to study these kind animals. This means that habitat destruction, hunting by humans, and natural predators such as jaguars were able to do their damage to the pacaranas before we even knew enough about them to take note.

Pacas

The paca, also known as the gibnut, is a brownish rodent about the size of a large rabbit with white spots along its back. It has the prized distinction of being the most coveted game animal of Belize and the Neotropics. Weighing in at about twenty-two pounds when fully grown (though it can grow up to forty pounds), the rodent averages two feet in length, plus a tail of about ten inches. Pacas are most often found near water, from river valleys to swamps to dense tropical forests. There they are able to exhibit their excellent swimming abilities. Nocturnal by habit, this solitary animal feeds on fallen fruit, leaves, and some tubers dug from the ground.

Unfortunately for the pacas, not only are they considered to be a tasty treat, but they are apparently easy to hunt as well. Dogs search out their dens by day while hunters use headlights to seek them out while they feed at night. Those threats are on top of the rodent's natural predators, which include the jaguar. As a result, the paca has been driven to extinction in many parts of its range from Mexico to southern Brazil, though they do continue to thrive in Belize's protected areas.

In many of those protected areas, pacas can be both heard and seen at night. The large rodent has proportionately large cheeks that help it make noises, such as hoarse barks or deep rumblings, which it often does when upset or provoked. Pacas also tend to make a scuffle when walking through dry leaves or while chewing on nuts.

Tuco-Tucos

The tuco-tuco is yet another South American rodent, hailing from the region stretching from Peru all the way down to Tierra del Fuego. They are named after the sound they make when they are frightened or defending their territory. Like the jird, there is more than just one form of this species. Scientists debate over the actual count, but the guess is that there are twenty-five to fifty different types of tuco-tucos. And although most of them choose to live in dry areas with sandy soil, at least one species lives in urban settings, and another would much rather live on the banks of streams.

Tuco-tucos average about six to ten inches in length, not including a tail of about two to four inches. They usually weigh between four and twenty-five ounces. Their eyes and ears are small, and their front teeth are protruding. The tuco-tuco's body is stocky and strong and is firmly held to the ground by feet that have special claws used for digging the elaborate tunnels and burrows in which the rodent lives. In addition to the claws, the animal also has stiff fringes of hair on its hind feet that act as combs to remove dirt from its fur! This fur that the tuco-tuco is so concerned about keeping clean is very thick, and it comes in a spectrum of colors ranging from light tan to black.

The tunnels and burrows dug by the tuco-tuco are highly elaborate and seemingly designed with community and family living in mind. They have chambers specifically for food storage, much like a human pantry, as well as separate rooms for raising the young, much like a human nursery. The rodent can even control the temperature of his home by opening and plugging tunnels. And because they have designed their homes so well in both form and function, the tuco-tucos rarely go far beyond the areas around the entrances of their burrows. In short, they are homebodies.

Female tuco-tucos give birth to only one litter per year, and depending on the species, gestation can last anywhere from 100 to 120 days, with litters of one to five young, though seven babies at a time are also possible. Maturity is reached after eight months, which is actually quite a large chunk of the rodent's two- to three-year life span.

Agoutis

Agouti is the common name for any of about a dozen species of rodents native to regions from southern Mexico down to Paraguay and Brazil, as well as the West Indies. They look like guinea pigs, as they are short-eared with practically no tail and have a soft coat of golden brown or reddish hair. Agouti hair is rather wiry, and individual hairs are banded in what is called "the agouti pattern." They have slender feet with long, hooflike claws. The larger forms of agouti can grow to be sixteen to twenty-four inches in length, though the average agouti is somewhat smaller.

Agoutis enjoy gnawing on roots, green leaves, and fruit, along with the occasional farm crop. One species of the rodent has even been known to eat crab. All agouti reproduce rather rapidly, with a gestation period of about three months. This means that a female can have more than one litter of one to three young each year. The babies, born open-eyed and with all of their fur, are more physically advanced and independent than most other baby mammals upon birth. They are even able to run at birth!

Indeed, if there is one thing the agouti can do, it is run. As rodents who eat crops and tend to damage sugarcane and banana plants, they often find themselves pursued by angry farmers. They are also used to being chased by hunters who are after their prized flesh. Fortunately for the rodent, the agouti are swift when they move about. But this alacrity is not to be taken for aggressiveness or offensiveness, as agouti are fairly shy animals. They live in underground dens and usually only come out in the day unless there are too many people around, in which case they become nocturnal.

Springhares

Springhares—also known as springhass, Jumping Hares, or Cape jumping hares—are a species of hopping African rodents native to the Kalahari desert. Do not be confused by their name, as they are not actually related to the hare. They have short forelegs and long, powerful hind legs and feet, actually making them seem more like miniature kangaroos than anything else. Springhares have even been known to bound ten to twenty feet in a single horizontal leap!

The average springhare can grow up to around eight to ten pounds. An adult is about fourteen to sixteen inches in length, not including a black-tipped tail that is usually as long as the rest of the body and is often used both for balance and as a brace when sitting. Other features are pointed ears and long, soft, light reddish brown or golden fur. The rodent also has beautifully large eyes that make it look both friendly and vulnerable at the same time.

Springhares are strictly nocturnal and only emerge out of their burrows at night to feed on roots and other vegetation. Sometimes when they leave the entrance of their burrow, they come bounding out almost like a kangaroo. Scientists' best guess at this behavior is that the rodent is trying to avoid any predators that might be waiting for it at the burrow opening.

These animals also tend to be well adapted for digging. Their front legs are each equipped with a small paw and five very long and curvy claws, which is an important feature, considering that they must dig their own tunnels and burrows to rest in during the day. In the wild, the rodents are nocturnal in habit and forage for bulbs, roots, grains, grasses, and insects. Conversely, springhares are a favorite and important food for the native people of South Africa. This might help explain why, though not considered to be endangered, they are considered to be a vulnerable African species.

They mate at any time of the year with a gestation of about eighty days. Usually one to two young are born at a time, and nursing goes on for about seven weeks. Mothers often rebreed while they are still nursing their newborns, resulting in three or four litters per year. A springhare in captivity can live up to fifteen years.

Animals That People Think Are Rodents but Are Not

Ferrets

How many of you readers would be willing to bet money that a ferret was a rodent? Considering their appearance and what we know about rodents in general, it might seem like a safe bet. But think again. The ferret is actually a member of the weasel family. Wild members of this family include mink, otters, and badgers. Ferrets themselves are basically domestic animals (there are no wild ferrets in the United States), and taxonomically, they are classified between cats and dogs. Domestication of the ferret occurred even before that of the cat and was thought to have been first done by the Egyptians. Lest you are still tempted to call a ferret a rodent, consider this: ferrets first came to the

United States over three hundred years ago on ships—to be used for rodent control!

Rabbits

Rabbits are most definitely not rodents. They do not share the same overall body structure or evolutionary history. Rabbits are lagomorphs, belonging to the family Leporidae. While there may be sixty-three species of lagomorphs worldwide, that's really nothing when you compare that to the more than 1,600 species of rodents. Keep in mind that

the order Roden-
tia is the largest
group of mammals
in the world. One of the
reasons why classifying
rabbits can be confusing is that
in pet stores they are often associated and confused with guinea
pigs. Their dentition, which you know is key to rodents, is
different from that of rodents, as are many other characteristics. Rabbits and hares also have extremely powerful
and large hind legs and feet, which provide a springboard
for their well-known movements.

Bats

Since bats are the only mammals that can fly, this puts
them in a league of their own. One of the only things that
rodents and bats have in common is that they are both
feared by humans. But their similarities are few. Both rodents and rats are nocturnal and have poor eyesight for
the most part. But bats' wings are their most distinctive
feature and sets them apart from rodents as well as many
other creatures. Instead of burrowing like rodents, bats
like to get a little rest and relaxation by retiring to caves or
trees to hang upside down.

Hedgehogs

You'll find most hedgehogs in the same places you'll find squirrels, such as backyards, parks, and farmlands. What do these three places have in common? Access to food. These creatures eat worms, slugs, beetles, and eggs, but unlike most rodents, they don't seek vegetation. Although hedgehogs are related to moles and shrews and not rodents, it is easy to watch their behavior and mistake them for rodents. As you know, one of the major characteristics of rodents is their ability to dig and burrow, and hedgehogs burrow as well. In fact their name reflects their tendency to burrow in hedgerows. A red flag that hedgehogs aren't rodents: they eat mice.

Shrews

Shrews have features similar to those of mice, making it easy to see why they are often mistaken for rodents. Belonging to the family Soricidae, shrews are not rodents. Despite being nocturnal, tiny—measuring as little as two inches long, the tail included—and having sharp teeth, these creatures are not related to rodents, rather they share a bond with hedgehogs. Their eating habits are similar to that of hedgehogs, as they both enjoy dining on insects and mice. Shrews can be found in North and Central America, Europe, Asia, and parts of South America.

Raccoons

Raccoons don't wreak as much havoc in your gardens as gophers, but they can become bothersome in your yard, specifically in your garbage cans. Since they are omnivores they will eat just about anything that has an appealing scent. They have grayish brown fur, a bushy tail, and tell-tale mask. Depending on access to food, raccoons can weigh up to sixty pounds, but the average weight range is fifteen to thirty. They usually set up shop in trees and enjoy living in forested areas. Their front paws are unique because they are similar to human hands with five dexterous digits. This makes lifting the lid of your trash can effortless.

Opossums

The opossum that is commonly found in the northern and southeastern United States resembles an oversized rat. But being marsupials, female opossums have a feature that rats don't have: a pouch. This pouch carries the mother's young, where they nurse for a three-month period. The litters can range anywhere from five to twenty offspring. Opossums are omnivorous and pose a greater threat to chicken coops than to gardens.

4

Attack of the Rodents: When Your Home Becomes Their Home

How to Tell If You Have a Problem

You wake up in the middle of the night to the sound of tiny feet pitter pattering—behind the walls. You've labored over your summer garden and now you are ready to reap the benefits of your hard work, but as you stand over your garden you realize that someone or something has already beaten you to your peas. You open your kitchen cabinets and see a trail of droppings from your box of favorite cereal to the hole in the wall. These are just a few of the telltale signs that you are sharing your living quarters with unwanted four-legged pests. You might even see one scurry past your feet in broad daylight. What most people learn shortly after the initial sighting is that where there is one rodent, many others will follow.

When it comes to determining if you have a mouse problem, the signs are usually apparent. It would be difficult to miss mouse droppings, or ignore the sounds of running, gnawing, squeaking, and clawing behind the walls. One of the most obvious signs that you have mice in your home is the presence of gnawed objects and areas, such as boxes or holes in walls. But you might not notice foot-marks in dirt and dust, or urine stains—these are trickier and make it more difficult to detect the intruder. Keep your eyes open for rodent nests. These hideaways are usu-ally made of soft, comfy, cozy and warm materials, such as fabric, grass, and shredded paper. Rodent nests most often are found in well-protected areas like inside and under furniture and appliances, inside boxes and cabinets.

There are ways to determine if you have an active ro-dent infestation. A red flag indicating you have a rodent problem in progress is the presence of fresh, glistening, black droppings. Dry, hard pellets mean they are old and might indicate a former problem. Since rodents urinate while on the run, streaks of urine are usually present as well. It is more difficult for the naked eye to determine if the urine streaks are fresh, but with the help of ultraviolet light, the freshness of the streaks is easily revealed.

Rodents gnaw daily as part of their dental maintenance regimen and as a means of survival. They will chew through wooden walls, posts, cabinets, and almost any-thing else to gain entry into your home or to get to a food source. If the wood is light in color and the chewed edges are sharp and splintery, then it is a recent incident. If the edges of the wood are dark and smooth, then it is an older case.

Being the creatures of habit that they are, rats tend to use the same paths from their living quarters to their food source daily. This means that tracking their footmarks should be fairly simple. Indoor paths usually are found alongside walls, while outdoor paths are more difficult to locate under vegetation. If the paths are dusty and carry cobwebs then they are no longer in operation. One way to determine if you have an active problem is to lay down a tracking powder. If you notice footmarks or tail drag trails, then you have an active rat problem.

There is no denying an infestation when you actually see the live rodent. If you find a stiff corpse and you no longer detect any rodent activity for nearly a fourteen-day period, then you might have *had* a problem. But if you see one run past you, then you know you've got a problem on your hands.

When You Live in an Apartment

Dealing with a rodent problem in an apartment building is a tricky affair. Your apartment might be immaculate, but all it takes is one careless tenant to bring down the whole complex. Whether you live in an apartment or own a home, the warning signs are the same. Rodents don't discriminate. You will find droppings, urine stains, chewed containers, and wrappers. You will hear scurrying and squeaking. And with a little detective work you will find the hole they use to get into your home.

According to Mark Greenleaf, program director for the Department of Health's Environmental Health Administration, rats "tend to be worse where there is an abundant domestic food supply at commercial sources and apartment buildings."

When David Ridgeway moved into his Washington, D.C., apartment he was told there wasn't a rodent problem. It took only one night in his new apartment for Ridgeway to figure out that that was exactly what he had on his hands. In the middle of the night he heard something large run by his bed. The second clue came the next day when he saw the alleyway outside of his apartment teeming with rats.

"You could hear them behind the walls. . . . There was knocking in the walls. It was very loud," he said. "If you kicked the walls it would stop. You could see them. You could go upstairs into our neighbor's home and see them in the yard."

Most apartment buildings in major cities are located near alleyways, which are hotbeds of rodent activity. Alleys usually house Dumpsters and tend to be dark and damp—two things mice and rats love. You will learn in the next chapter that with the proper maintenance and protocol Dumpsters do not have to contribute to multiplying the rodent population. Nearby restaurants that were not properly disposing of their trash also contributed to the rat problem in Ridgeway's neighborhood. But the rats were getting into his apartment via a hole in the ground that was connected to a drainpipe.

"We had a guy to the house, one of the contractors, he said the problem was that the rats are in the alleyway and they are eating at the big Dumpsters and on the way back they are hitting our little garbage cans. Because the city won't give us the big green cans with the lids, they drop off there for a little snack and then they go into our yards and burrow there and get into our buildings through pipes and into our kitchens," Ridgeway said.

He started a full-fledged assault on the rats.

I started trying myself. I plugged up the holes with steel wool. That didn't work. They ate through it or moved it. Then I called the [building managers]. They sent someone over and they put down poison. I called the city and they gave me film to take pictures of trash in the area. . . . Nothing changed. . . . The rats were about eight to twelve inches long and they weren't scared of people. They didn't run away. . . . I bought a huge rat trap, and put out the trap with rotten meat on it. At about two in the morning, the trap went off and there was a little bit of movement. Ten seconds later there was this rumbling, thrashing around. The cabinet doors were bouncing around and slamming shut. The rat wormed its way out of the trap. It was like the exorcist had entered my home. I went to the kitchen and grabbed the steak knife and tried to stab it and it was running around and it slipped through the hole and ran away.

Eventually Ridgeway's landlords cemented the entire backyard, making it impossible for the rats to dig and burrow. His neighbors had to cut down a nearby tree, since there were rats living in it. At one point, contractors found between fifteen and thirty rat nests in the tree, Ridgeway says. He has not seen a rat in about two months.

When someone in the district calls the rodent division, the office takes down the name and address. The division dispatches workers to go to the premises, but the entire area is then inspected. The next step is to assess the area in question, check for proper rodent proofing, then make referrals for enforcement. Mark Greenleaf says it is key to change the behavior of residences and businesses. "We want them to stop littering and feeding pigeons in the park," he says. This is difficult, however, because in the District of Columbia there are many visitors who don't know the harm they are doing by feeding birds. The final word according to Greenleaf: "The baiting and the other stuff is good, but ultimately you need to change the behavior."

When Your Home Is a House

City dwellers who live in apartments are not the only ones fending off mice and rats. Homeowners in the suburbs are also in the position to be victimized. Remember, rodents do not discriminate. One of the benefits of owning the home in which you have a rodent problem is that you alone are in charge of your destiny. You don't have to depend on your next-door neighbors' cleanliness or lack thereof. The negative side, however, is that you might have a lot more ground to cover if you own a large home and property.

Seven months after moving into their single-family home on a third of an acre about fifteen miles outside of Washington, D.C., Bridget Cooper and her husband made some unusual sightings.

"We saw black droppings on our kitchen counters, and after we would remove them, they would be back in similar places the following day. After a day or two of this, we noticed that chocolate bars [in wrappers] and brownies in plastic wrap had been gnawed on by little teeth," Cooper wrote in an E-mail message.

The culprit: mice. The means: a hole in the floorboard underneath the kitchen sink. The remedy:

We scoured the kitchen and removed any and all food items from the counters and accessible pantry areas. We closed off the obvious entry points to the house [gaps around faucets] from the outside and from the floorboards to the sink area, first with a steel wool look-alike, and then with true steel wool. The former failed. The latter worked. My husband awoke to hear the mouse one night and he found it in the trash can, so he took it outside and put it in our Dumpster. The next night a mouse was back in the house, so we assumed that he escaped or he had a partner in crime. We set one trap and caught the mouse and never had the problem again.

After their experience with mice, Cooper offers these words of wisdom:

Fill all gaps to the home with caulking, steel wool, or something nonporous. Check for gaps/ holes within the house, particularly under sinks, and fill them also. If the mice have found their way in the house, set traps (near entry points). I don't like to kill animals, but we tried the preventive way and that didn't work and they were very determined to be in our house, so we concluded that it was our best option. I would also recommend that people ensure that their kitchens, etc., are clean and that their food items are stored in strong containers that cannot be chewed through by rodents . . . to prevent the enticement of things like cookies and things that might be accessible.

It's important to note that the Cooper's mouse problem is a minor example of the damage that mice can cause. Although their mouse problem pales in comparison to infestations that other homeowners have to deal with, the methods they employed can be used for all situations. Whether you have two or twenty mice scurrying through your home, there are some tried and true methods that will most often do the trick.

Dangers of Rodent Infestation

You might think that the worst part of a rodent problem is the overwhelming inconvenience. Unfortunately, things can get worse. Rodents can not only cause tremendous damage to your property and peace of mind, but they also can pose a serious health risk. Over the years, mice and rats have proven to be successful vehicles of a host of diseases, including the deadly hantavirus pulmonary syndrome (HPS), the plague, and histoplasmosis.

The elderly, the disabled, and young children are the most common victims of rodent bites. In addition to keeping their kitchens and eating areas clean, caretakers and parents should wash bedding and clothes frequently. Most rat attacks on infants, for example, occur because the rats smell milk on the baby and the crib.

Hantavirus Pulmonary Syndrome

Hantavirus pulmonary syndrome (HPS) is one of the most recently recognized rodent-related diseases to surface in North America. Infection occurs when a person comes in contact with droppings from a rodent—the most common carrier being the deer mouse—carrying hantaviruses. It is a potentially deadly disease that requires immediate treatment and care once symptoms develop. Initial signs of illness are fever and muscle aches that appear one to five weeks after infection. When coughing and shortness of breath begin, hospitalization and ventilation soon follow.

Deer mice, cotton rats, and rice rats, all three of which are found in the Southeast, and white-footed mice in the Northeast are the most common rodents infected with the specific type of hantavirus that causes cases of HPS in the United States. Although the common house mouse does not carry hantavirus, any of the rodents that do are capable of finding their ways into homes. The virus exits the system of its host through its bodily fluids, including its droppings, urine, and saliva. Infection usually occurs when these substances are disturbed and the virus is released into the air, which is called aerosolization. People can contract the disease by inhaling contaminated air, but there are several other ways to become infected with the disease. Although it is rare, a person can contract the virus if he or she is bitten by an infected rodent. According to the National Center for Infectious Diseases, researchers believe a person may contract it by touching something that has been in contact with infected urine, feces, or saliva and then passing it on to his or her nose and mouth. There is also the chance of catching the virus through foods that have been contaminated by the virus. The good news is that the kinds of hantaviruses that cause HPS cannot be transmitted from person to person.

According to the National Institute for Disease Control, as of May 8, 2000, there have been 250 reported cases of HPS in the United States since the disease was first spotted in May 1993. About 40 percent of the cases resulted in death. Most of the western half of the United States and a small number of eastern states account for the thirty-one states where cases have been reported.

While you cannot catch the disease from your pet dog or cat, they can bring a diseased mouse or rat to your doorstep. If your pet brings you such a "gift," you should follow the following protocol for disposing of it. After you put on rubber gloves, spray the dead animal and the surrounding area thoroughly with disinfectant. Take a resealable plastic bag large enough to accommodate the rodent and fill it about two-thirds full with disinfectant. Put the rodent inside the bag and seal it. Since you can never be too careful when it comes to handling diseased animals, put it in another bag and seal it also. Follow the same guidelines for disposing of any materials the dead animal might have touched.

The next step is getting rid of the materials. Your options are burning the bags outside, burying the bags in a four-foot-deep hole, or calling your local state health department and requesting that they dispose of it.

Here are some other precautions you should take to avoid rodent-borne diseases:

- Clean a rodent-infested area by spraying disinfectant over every surface. Try to decrease the amount of dust floating around by mopping the floor first with a mixture of soap and disinfectant. To further prevent any chance of infection, wash everything down with a mixture of soap, detergent, and disinfectant. Let dry. Wash again with disinfectant only.
- Have carpets or furniture professionally cleaned. Launder your bedding or other fabrics in hot water with plenty of detergent, then dry on a high setting.
- Cook meats thoroughly, especially pork products. Rats and mice often live near swine, usually in the large grain troughs. Pigs eat the rodents' droppings or the rodents themselves, thereby ingesting *Trichinella spiralis,* the tiny worm that causes trichinosis in humans. The pigs become infected with the disease, are slaughtered, and then the meat is passed

on to consumers. Proper cooking ensures the killing of all dangerous parasites, so cook any pork product thoroughly, as well as freeze any leftovers promptly.

The Plague

Bubonic plague wiped out millions of people in Europe during the Middle Ages, but much like the rats responsible for spreading the disease, the plague lives on, posing a modern threat. The spread of a disease as destructive as the plague is not solely the work of rats. Most cases are caused by rats and rat fleas carrying the bacterium *Yersinia pestis*. When a flea feeds on the blood of an infected rat and the rat dies, the flea goes in search of another host. The flea also will die, about three days after it is infected, but that gives it plenty of time to infect another rat or a human being.

The most common symptom associated with the plague is a swollen, tender lymph gland called a "bubo," hence the name bubonic. Other signs of the plague are pain, chills, fever, headache, and fatigue. These symptoms occur around two to six days after becoming infected. If a person infected with the plague does not get immediate medical attention, such as antibiotic therapy, plague-related bacteria multiply in the bloodstream, resulting in a serious and sometimes fatal condition. According to the Division of Vector-Borne Infectious Diseases, about 14 percent of cases of the plague in the United States end in death.

In 1994, India battled a plague outbreak. The most recent outbreak of the plague in the United States occurred in Los Angeles in 1924 to 1925. But cases still arise in rural areas and cities where undomesticated rodents infected with the plague are running wild and free. Nowadays, the plague afflicts about ten to fifteen people annually in the United States. According to the World Health Organization one thousand to three thousand cases are reported worldwide every year. In the United States, the plague rears its ugly head in only two regions: southern Colorado, northern Arizona, northern New Mexico and California, southern Oregon, and western Nevada.

The first step you should take with any rodent-related problem is rodent proofing your home, which you will learn about in the following chapter. More disease-specific precautions include using insect repellents to prevent flea bites; wearing gloves when in contact with infected animals; keeping your pet dogs and cats from frequenting high-risk areas and treating them for flea control; and using chemical treatments to wipe out fleas in specific areas during outbreaks. In addition to antibiotics, there is a vaccine that is recommended for professionals in contact with plague bacterium in the laboratory setting or people in contact with infected animals.

Histoplasmosis

Histoplasmosis is less serious than the bubonic plague and HPS but still has the potential to cause serious problems in the nervous and respiratory systems. The histoplasmosis fungus is carried in rodent feces. Common symptoms of the disease are lingering coldlike symptoms, achiness, and a feeling of general malaise.

According to Jake Kellio of Santa Cruz, California, he and his roommate had their own brush with histoplasmosis, but since the symptoms are sometimes mild they did not know until they did a little digging. Here is his story:

A couple years ago, my friend and I lived on the second floor of a house in Knoxville, Tennessee. We knew we had mice because we saw their droppings in the kitchen near the fridge. Then we saw droppings along the shelves near there. I realized that they were climbing up the handle of the broom. Anyway, we bought some d-Con and put it all around there. Problem solved, or so I thought.

My friend and I both worked in the food industry, so neither of us were particularly surprised that we had slight colds the entire time we lived in that house. It was never bad like the flu, but we each had stuffed-up noses and bad coughs most of the time. We attributed it to the germs floating around our jobs and heavy smoking, and drank a lot of orange juice. When the time came to move out, we couldn't believe what we found in hidden places all over our apartment: mice droppings. We found them behind the VCR and television set, inside the pull-out bed in the couch, and—worse of all—on a windowsill near one of our beds. That explained an awful lot. I know now that we probably had a low-grade case of histoplasmosis.

5

Strategies for Eliminating Them

*How to Make Sure You Never Get Them—
or Get Them Back*

The cardinal rule of rodent control is *get rid of the food source.* The reason rodents, especially mice and rats, are attracted to a location in the first place is because they can find the three things they need the most to survive: water, food, and shelter. Untied garbage bags, trash cans with no lids, open cereal boxes, and crumbs on the countertop are open invitations that say to rodents, "Come in and make yourselves right at home. I think you'll find your stay here enjoyable. How else can we accommodate you?" The thing is that these guests do not know when to leave, and they tend to bring others along with them. Remember that even if the problem appears to be restricted to the outdoors, most likely your rodents will find a way inside your home. Often frustrated homeowners head for the hardware store and purchase the first poison bait they can find.

Poison baits can be effective *if* you implement strict rodent control prevention methods first and foremost.

When confronted with a rodent problem, a homeowner initially should inspect his or her property during daylight, paying special attention to areas that might attract or harbor rodents. In California, the City of Fremont's Police Department's Animal Services recommends that you take these precautions in your yard:

- Keep lids on trash cans.
- Feed birds only in areas where food can be cleaned immediately.
- Feed pets only the amount they will eat—no leftovers!
- Remove pet droppings from yard.
- Trim or cut down thick vegetation near house.
- Store firewood off the ground—do not lean it against buildings or fences.
- Keep the doors to sheds closed tightly.
- Harvest ripe food sources like fruit and nut trees and vegetable plants.
- Check all areas for rat droppings.

Fremont also offers a few pointers on how to keep the rodents from entering your home:

- Replace loose-fitting crawl space covers with tight-fitting ones.

- Seal openings around cables, pipes, and wires that lead to your home.
- Fix damaged ventilation screens.
- Put weather stripping around garage doors so that they close tightly.
- Seal holes in aging wood stairs with quarter-inch galvanized screen.

Landscaping

Landscaping plays an integral role in rodent control. If you allow the vegetation in your yard to grow wild, then you might be helping mice and rats create their own hideout. If there is a nearby food source, rodents will find shelter close by, where they will live and breed. When choosing plants to put in your yard or garden try to stay away from plants that bear large amounts of fruit or seeds. You also should avoid plants that have thick, dense foliage. Instead, choose plants with sparser foliage and space them apart from one another. You will want to keep any bushes or shrubs at least two to three feet away from walls, such as the base of your home or shed. The District of Columbia's Environmental Health Administration (EHA) recommends laying down a border of pea stones or gravel along the walls. The border should be approximately four to six inches deep and one foot wide. Mowing your lawn frequently and removing weeds as soon as they sprout helps

keep problem areas exposed and deters rodents from burrowing in those areas. Spreading stone or gravel throughout shrub areas is also recommended. Shrubs should be
trimmed often so that limbs do not cover the ground.
When bushes are trimmed properly and regularly, it becomes easier to inspect the area for rodent habitation.
Check your yard weekly for rodent activity. To determine if
a burrow is currently in use, place an object in the opening
and check it the following day. If the object is gone or disturbed then you might have an active burrow on your
hands.

Garbage

The District of Columbia's Environmental Health Administration recommends using metal or heavy plastic containers with tight lids to store trash. Another tip is putting
out the trash shortly before it is to be picked up to avoid
leaving garbage bags outdoors overnight, which is when
mice and rats are the busiest. For rural homeowners, make
frequent trash disposal runs. Make sure there are enough
garbage receptacles around eating areas, and place them
in open areas, far away from walls.

Some people use compactors as a way to more effi-
ciently manage their garbage. According to the EHA, non-
rodent-proof compactors can signal bad news if there are
rodents in the area, so they have designed guidelines for

those in the market for a compactor or current owners of the devices:

- Unit should be watertight.
- The loading door should have a rubber seal on all of its sides.
- When dealing with medical or fish wastes, a mist applicator should be used to minimize odors.
- Use thicker PVC belting—one-half instead of one-quarter inch thick.
- The door should be kept tightly shut when not in use.
- Clean areas surrounding the compactor daily.
- Replace gaskets every two to five years.
- Check for possible rodent entryways periodically.

Dumpsters

When walking through the alleyways of almost any major city it is not uncommon to see or hear rodents scurrying through a Dumpster. This is probably one of the most common images people associate with mice and rats. In many cases, the Dumpster is filled to capacity or brimming over with trash. The bags are untied and ripping, garbage is exposed, and the smell of rotten food is in the air—a rodent's paradise. The first step to correcting poor Dumpster etiquette is keeping lids and doors shut tightly to bar rodents from entering the Dumpster, and to prevent trash from spilling out of it. Since rats can climb concrete walls and are good jumpers, it is wise to place Dumpsters away from walls and other vertical surfaces. Dumpsters should not be placed on soil because rodents burrow in the earth, making it convenient for them to live right underneath their food source. Instead, Dumpsters should be located on pavement. Since Dumpsters tend to rust along the bottom corners, make sure they are made of strong metal or heavy-duty plastic. Rust signals the beginning of a hole, and any opening one-quarter of an inch or larger is a portal for a mouse. The area surrounding a Dumpster should be cleaned daily. If you clean the area with a hose, make sure the water empties into a drain. You do not want to leave puddles because they can become a rodents' potential water source.

The good news is that if you follow these rodent-proofing methods you should be on your way to guarding against rodent problems or at least minimizing them. The bad news is that the battle is not over once you take away the rodent's food source. You still have more work to do.

Good Housekeeping

A clean home is a happy—and potentially rodent-free—home. This might seem like an obvious statement, but you would be surprised to find out how opportunistic mice and rats are when it comes to living off what you might consider a small amount of food. To you, a cookie crumb means nothing. To a mouse, a cookie crumb could be the meal du jour. To skeptics this seems like an exaggeration, but any person who has battled a mouse problem will stress how important it is to make sure everything in your home is food- and dirt-free. This applies mainly to the kitchen area but does not exclude other areas where food is present. If mice know they can get even a crumb in your home, they will come back for more, so try not to whet their appetites with tiny morsels of food. This can be accomplished by sweeping floors and cleaning counters, sinks, stove tops, and garbage areas regularly. In extreme cases, it is important to take action as soon as you are finished cooking or eating food. That means, don't let your plate of leftovers sit on the table while you watch the evening news. There is no such thing as cleaning up *later.* Waiting until after the evening news could be too late. By then, your plate might be clean, but not by you or any other human being. Remember, the point is to feed yourself and starve the mice.

The scent of food, especially rotting garbage, can send a strong message to rodents in the area. If you are walking by a restaurant and you smell an irresistible aroma wafting through the air, what do you do? Nine times out of ten you will turn around and follow the scent to see where it is coming from. Rodents are no different from us in that respect. Strong odors can attract legions of mice to your home, so never leave trash around long enough to develop a stench. You should dispose of trash immediately. If the problem is serious, don't wait until the trash is completely full. You'll feel a lot better if you take the trash out after you clean, and always use a disinfectant to remove any harmful bacteria and odors. Using Tupperware also can help in two ways. Tupperware seals in odors better than most containers. What the rodents can't smell, they might not find. Also, Tupperware is more difficult for mice and rats to nibble through.

'Tis the Season

It is crucial to stay one step ahead of the enemy at all times. When dealing with rodents, this means knowing when to expect them. It might seem as though they come into your homes and yards whenever they choose, but their patterns of behavior are directly related to the changing seasons. So in order to be on the defensive rather than the offensive, you have to know exactly what the season is bringing your way.

The good news is that rodent populations and breeding patterns are at their lowest during winter. Many rodents have a difficult time braving extended periods of cold and snow. Since natural food sources, like insects and seeds, are no longer in abundance during this season, rodents have a difficult task finding food. The bad news is that during the winter months rodents that are lurking about tend to seek warm, cozy places near or inside buildings. When the first cold spell hits, mice and rats waste no time finding a place to stay warm. During the winter you will not have to worry about rodents digging up your garden or hanging out in your bushes, but you will have to worry about them being close to your home, if not inside it. They will head for your homes, sheds, and other places for shelter when the cold front sweeps through. If the winter is mild, don't count on seeing a tremendous drop-off in the rodent population, as fewer of them will die from natural causes. The more rodents that are around during the winter means that there will be even more of them during spring. Winter is the most crucial time to start controlling rodents, since the way you handle the problem can determine the type of rodent activity you will have the rest of the year.

Rodents seem to catch spring fever just like human beings. As the weather gets warmer during March, yearly breeding cycles get under way, which translates into litters upon litters of newborn mice and rats looking for food and a place to call home. Things begin to look brighter for mice and rats during spring because spring showers mean that vegetation is growing, which provides them with a place to breed and sources of food.

According to the D.C. Department of Health's Environmental Health Administration, mice and rat sightings are at their highest from April to June as a result of increased breeding that occurs during the spring months. The other prolific period is during October and November.

During the summer, mice and rats are in abundance as a result of the good breeding conditions during spring. Since vegetation is full and lush, mice and rats are given the added bonus of having more places to hide, breed, and eat. If the summer turns out to be a wet one, weeds will grow offering shelter. A rainy summer also provides more water and food sources, thereby increasing the rodent population.

As the weather begins to cool down and vegetation starts to dry up, rodents are still in abundance, but the population is on a downward swing during fall. There is much less activity in gardens and diminished interest in vegetation as rodents start looking for shelter in preparation for winter, and then the cycle starts all over again.

Methods

Now that you know the best methods to *prevent* a rodent problem, you must know the way to tackle the worst case scenario. You hear the scurrying behind the walls; you see fresh droppings; you notice all of the telltale signs of a rodent problem. Whether you feel as though there is only one persistent mouse, or you have a rat infestation, you come to the decision that you want to be rodent-free once and for all. So what do you do? There are many factors in deciding the kind of methods you want to use. First and foremost, you must determine which type of rodent you are battling. Methods you use to trap a mouse might not be useful against a rat, mainly because of their physical differences. Next you should determine whether you have a serious rodent infestation or a mild case. You also should consider what you want to do with the rodent once it has been caught. You should decide if you want to kill and dispose of it, or just catch it and send it packing—alive.

The most common method of catching rodents is the trap. The most common household trap is the snap trap. Other common methods include glue boards, live-catch traps, and rodenticides. The live-catch traps are designed to catch individual rodents, but some are made to catch multiple rodents.

Mice and Rats

Snap Traps

Of all the traps available commercially, people are most familiar with snap traps, which are regarded as one of the most humane ways to capture a rodent. The base of the traditional snap trap is a rectangular, wood foundation. The other part is a metal or plastic spring bar, which is usually pulled back and held in place with a locking bar. The locking bar goes into the hole in the trigger. A small amount of pressure on the trigger will release the spring and the metal or plastic bar will snap the neck or spine of the rodent, causing death instantly in most cases.

This seems like a fairly simple process. All you need to do is get a trap, put it down on the floor, flip the spring bar, secure it in the trigger, and wait for the critter to walk into the trap, right? Not exactly. It's going to take a little more of a strategy to get a mouse or rat into that trap.

When you go to purchase your traps, you should buy more than one, at least three per room. The more traps you have around the room, the better your chances of nabbing your rodent. The traps should be set in areas where you know there is rodent activity. Mice and rats rarely hang out in the middle of rooms, waiting to be spotted. They usually make their way around your homes alongside walls, which is where you should place the traps. You should also try to locate any holes that might serve as entryways. Place traps as close as possible to these openings, as well as behind any objects or in dark, hidden corners. When setting up a trap near a wall, position the trap with the bait hook facing the wall.

When baiting traps, you must pay special attention to your choice of cuisine. What appeals to a mouse might not necessarily appeal to a rat. Bait choices for mice include peanut butter, cookies, dried fruits, nuts, cheese, cooked bacon, gumdrops, chocolate bars, raw meat, and oatmeal. Norway rats cannot seem to resist bits of bacon and pieces of hot dogs. You can also buy bait pellets. It is not necessary to put a large amount of food on the trap. You don't want to feed the rodent. Instead, you want to put only enough food so that it will send out a scent to attract it to your trap. When putting down the trap, it is important that you do not touch around the area more than you have to.

You want the rodent to smell only the scent of the bait, not your scent. There are some snap traps that come equipped with a larger trigger, making it easy for the rodent to set off the trap. Since the trigger is larger, it is not necessary to use bait with these traps. But if you want to use all of your resources, bait away, as it certainly can't hurt.

Now that you have purchased the snap trap and have figured out how it operates and where you are going to put it, you have to exercise a little restraint and sit tight. Instead of immediately baiting and setting the trap, you should put the trap in the desired spot unset but baited. This way, the rodents will become familiar with the trap and will not view it as dangerous. Not only will they become comfortable with it, but they will also seek it, since they know they can count on it as a food source. Keep the unset trap out for a few consecutive days. Think of it as a card game. You don't want to show your opponent your hand. By making them feel safe around the trap, you will reduce the chance of training the rodents to be trap shy. After the bait has disappeared for a few consecutive days, set the traps.

Keep several traps out in various locations for an extended period of time—at least two weeks. You should check your traps every morning—since mice and rats are nocturnal creatures—to see if you've captured your critter. If you have not caught a rodent after three days, then it is time to move your traps around and put fresh bait on them. To improve your chances of catching a mouse or rat, place the traps on a piece of cardboard. If you want to drive mice out of their crevices and into your traps, apply peppermint to a cotton ball and place it in the entryway of their nest site. Mice hate the smell, so hopefully it will drive them out of their hiding place and into your trap. If the rate at which you are catching rodents in your trap slows down, this could be an indicator that your problem has slowed down. Once you stop finding rodents in your trap over a two-week period you can celebrate. Empty traps are usually an indicator that rodent activity has come to a close. However, once rodents see several of their former friends on the trap, they get the picture and avoid the trap at all costs. So when dealing with large infestations, snap traps are not as effective as other methods.

Disposing of the Snap-Trapped Rodent

If you are sure the rodent is dead, then you should proceed with a burial you see fit. Just to be safe, you should use rubber gloves when disposing of any rodent. Either remove the body from the trap or throw away the entire trap. Since snap traps are reusable, you might want to hold on to it in case you have a future rodent problem. But if picking up a rodent, that is voluntarily touching it, is out of the question, then bid the trap farewell. In both cases, put the material into a plastic bag and then into the garbage.

Note: Precise measures for disposal of diseased rodents are described on pages 87–88. If there have been outbreaks of rodent-borne illnesses in your area, please follow these instructions.

Unfortunately, it is not always that simple. You should prepare yourself for some gruesome situations. Snap traps have been known to leave rodents completely mutilated. Sometimes snap traps do not kill the rodent upon impact. Instead, the rodents are stuck in the trap—alive. This leaves you with a difficult decision to make. If the rodent does not appear to be seriously injured, release it into a deserted area far, far away from your home—at least half a mile away. But if the rodent is seriously injured, it might be in the best interest of the rodent for you to finish the job. Learn2.com suggests that one way of euthanizing a rodent is to put the rodent in an airtight jar for about twenty-four hours. Since mice and rats can survive a long time in a closed container, make sure the jar is not too large. The less oxygen in the jar, the quicker the rodent will be put out of its misery.

It is important to note that snap traps pose a safety risk when children and pets are present. So try to put them in inaccessible areas where your children and pets can't find them. Getting a hand or a paw caught in a snap trap can be a painful experience, resulting in broken bones.

Glue Boards

Glue boards are considered one of the most inhumane ways to solve a rodent problem and are therefore one of the least popular methods of rodent control. Glue boards use a nondrying glue to capture both mice and rats. The rodent steps onto the board, gets stuck, and since it is unable to get to any water or food source, it dies. But the time between the moment the rodent gets stuck to the glue board and the moment it dies is guaranteed to be unpleasant. Mice and rats usually do not sit on the glue board quietly waiting to die. Instead, they have been known to start screaming—a loud, humanlike noise. They also tend to thrash about and quiver in an attempt to set themselves free. This leaves you with two options: disposing of a live rodent while it is stuck to the glue board, or waiting for it to die. The best thing to do is to make the rodent's death as quick as possible, which means you can either drown it in a bucket of water, or administer a quick blow to the head with a blunt object.

If you feel as though you can stomach either of those options, here's what you need to know. There are smaller standard-size glue boards designed for mice, and larger boards created for rats. If you try to catch a rat using a smaller glue board, the rat will most likely drag the board around your home. Although there are glue boards specially designed for rats, rats have been known to escape from these devices. With that in mind, you might want to rethink using these if you have a rat problem.

As with snap traps, the glue boards should be placed in areas where rodent activity is suspected. To insure the traps are being used in the most efficient manner, place several traps in each area, for example along walls or small runways. Do not place glue boards in areas where they can accumulate dust or get wet, as this will diminish their effectiveness. In order to keep the animal from dragging the board through your home, secure it with double-stick tape or a tack. Once the glue boards are in place all that you need to do is make sure they are baited. Depending on the brand, the traps might already come prebaited. If they are not, a sprinkle of birdseed will do the trick. Animaltraps.com offers Catchmaster glue boards designed for mice at five by eight inches, and Maxcatch glue boards for rats, measuring eighteen by ten inches.

In July 1985, the Association of Veterinarians for Animal Rights declared its opposition to the use of glue traps as a means to catch rodents or any other animal. According to the association, the traps are "inherently cruel and their use can never be justified." While the association acknowledges the fact that there are cases in which it is necessary to control the rodent population, it believes only those methods that are natural and nonlethal should be used. If the animal must be killed, the method should be quick and cause the animal as little pain as possible.

Live-Catch and Multiple-Catch Traps

Live-catch traps enable you to nab your intruder without killing it. So if you would prefer to keep your pests alive and in one piece, then this is the product for you. One of the benefits of using these traps is that since they do not harm the rodent, they do not fear it or become trap shy. Another benefit to live-catch traps is that they have the capacity to capture and hold several rodents at a time. While there are several live-catch traps on the market designed to capture a single rodent, most people prefer to use models that catch many rodents at a time. Remember, all of the traps mentioned in this chapter should be placed in areas where rodent activity is suspected, which in homes is usually around walls. These traps also can be used outdoors. Though using traps outdoors is an effective way of stopping them from entering your home, placing them in the right spot can be tricky. Inside of a home, you have four walls to line with traps, but in the great outdoors there are too many nooks and crannies to count.

The T101 Small Animal Trap is a ten-inch-long rectangular, sheet metal container designed to trap one small animal. These traps are not recommended for trapping rats but are useful for catching smaller creatures like mice, chipmunks, gerbils, and hamsters. The rodent is lured into the container by the bait already placed inside of it. The door to the device is folded down and serves as a trip pan, so that when the animal walks into the device it sets off the spring-activated door, which immediately closes behind it.

The Victor Tin Cat Live Trap is designed for mice. It has two entrances leading to a collapsible walkway that drops the mice into a holding area—think of it as a waiting room. To attract mice to the trap, you should place bait in the holding area, which can house up to twenty mice at a time.

If you do not intend to check the traps daily, you should place a substantial amount of bait in the trap. Sometimes people leave the traps in their home while they are on vacation, or they don't make frequent trips to their barnyards to check on the trap's progress. Whatever the case may be, it is important to provide the mice with a supply of food or else they will turn from quiet and calm rodents to trapped, frenzied captives. If left unattended, another possibility is death. Not only does this undermine your attempt to humanely solve the problem, but it also causes an odorous mess.

If you are putting your trap in a wet or damp area, the Kwik Katch Live Mouse Trap is ideal because it is plastic. It also operates with a windup mechanism, like the Mouse Master, but holds fewer mice, housing up to eight.

The first thing to remember when dealing with rats is that they need larger traps. A mousetrap won't work. You can get the best of both worlds with the TS550 live trap, which works as both a single and multicatch trap. All you need to do is bait the trip trap and wait for the rodent to come. When the trip trap is triggered by the rat's weight, the door to the cage will close. In order to trap more than one rat, you should set the trap with two bait stations: one in front of the tray and one behind it. This way, while the first rat is nibbling on the bait in front of the tray, the door to the cage stays open while another rat wanders in, forcing the first one to step back to the second bait, and setting off the trigger. One benefit of using this product is that even after the door is triggered shut, it can be pushed open from the outside because it is spring-loaded.

One thing you should consider before purchasing one of these contraptions is that once you've caught your creature, you still have to determine what you are going to do with it. You'll need either to drive miles away from your home to drop it off in the middle of a field, or you might want to make a kind contribution to your local pet store. A less popular option is submerging the trap in water to drown the rodents.

Baiting traps appears to be an effective tool if you have a minor problem, according to Mark

Greenleaf, program manager for the Department of Health's Environmental Health Administration. But in some areas, such as Washington, D.C., where rat problems are more serious, more preventive measures need to take place in order for the problem to improve. "It takes weeks or months to eliminate a problem, which is dependent on sanitation, food supply, and reduction. You can bait until you are blue in the face, you will kill lots of rats, but they will come back. It's a three-dimensional problem. We deal with the surface, and they are burrowing animals and you have to deal with the sewers," said Greenleaf. He says that the rat problem has been serious for the last three to four years in the district, and since the early 1980s it has gotten worse. Due to federal funding cuts for rodent control, the cities had to pick up the burden, which they were not prepared to do financially.

Ultrasonic Devices

The jury is still out on whether or not these devices really work on rodents. But that doesn't stop manufacturers from claiming that when rodents pick up these sound frequencies they run. Sonic Technology manufactures one of the most popular lines of ultrasonic devices called the PestChaser. These devices emit sound waves in a range from thirty-two to sixty-two kilohertz, which is about 1,000 cycles per second. Rodents have the ability to hear sounds up to 100,000 cycles per second compared to humans, who hear only up to 20,000 cycles per second. The range of PestChaser is one that rodents hear clearly, but your pets, such as cats and dogs, cannot. These frequencies should not trigger other ultrasonic devices in your home, such as home security systems. Since the sounds do not pass through solid surfaces, it is necessary to put one in every room. Rodents can't stand these noises, so they will try to get as far away from the sound as possible, the idea being that they'll flee your home.

Rodenticides

Most pest control professionals recommend the use of rodenticides as a last resort. Mark Greenleaf recommends using only EPA-registered products by state or district licensed and certified companies to control rodents and only if it's a worst-case scenario. Rodenticides are poison baits that usually work as anticoagulants that prevent blood clotting and eventually lead to death. They are more appropriate for use in commercial buildings, sheds, abandoned structures, and generally anyplace where children and pets cannot access them. But if you have been unsuccessful with all other methods and feel as though your rodent infestation requires the use of poison, as with all of the materials and devices mentioned in this book, remember to read the directions to ensure your safety and the safety of those around you.

It's important to note that rodenticides work on both mice and rats and contain active ingredients that ensure the rodent will die after consuming a single dose. One of these products is Contrac. Since it comes in several different forms, you must decide which kind suits your needs. According to U-Spray, Contrac Cakes are designed for outdoor use, but can be used indoors. Since they are weather resistant, they can be used in damp basements or wet outdoor burrows. For indoor treatments use Contrac Pellets. Med-Pest Control offers another alternative in Ditrac Rat & Mouse Bait, which contains Diphacinone, which is another anticoagulant but uses fewer chemicals to kill rats and mice. You can find many kinds of rat poisons at your local hardware store. To get rodents familiar with the area, put out food that is not poisoned. This will get them comfortable, and they will not fear the poisoned food when you put it out.

When using rodenticides be prepared to find dead rodents in random places. Since they do not die immediately after consumption you never know where they will be when the poison begins to take effect. There is the possibility that rodents will go back to their living quarters behind your walls or under your home, where they will die unnoticed until you smell the odor. The next big problem is getting the dead corpse from behind the wall, which is a job only a professional can do.

The city of Chicago, which has worked on getting its rat problem under control for some time now, has found relative success in rodenticides. "We've pretty much maintained our rat population over the past six years, and controlled the population by using rodenticides," said John Antonacci, general superintendent and director at the Bureau of Rodent Control in Chicago. "Now, rodenticides aren't working because the areas that have problems are producing more garbage. We want [the rats] to eat the poison, not the food." Antonacci says that what makes this program different from any other in the country is that Chicago is the only city that has a rodent control bureau housed within the Department of Streets and Sanitation, rather than the Health Department. "The problem is that the Health Department is so inundated with so many other issues, that they can't focus on the [rodent] issue," he says.

Umbrellas

And to think, you thought umbrellas were useful only on rainy days. I wouldn't suggest using the umbrella method as your first form of rodent trapping. But if you have a little mouse in your house and you're up for a little exercise and enjoy teamwork, then this might be just what you need. This method requires two people, an umbrella, a magazine, and a pair of running shoes. First you have to keep watch and always be prepared with a magazine and an umbrella on hand. When you spot the unsuspecting mouse, get behind it with a magazine as though you were pushing it forward or at least blocking its retreat. Guide the mouse into the *open* umbrella. Once the mouse runs into the umbrella, shut it immediately and tie the top. Now you have a mouse in your umbrella, and you can do with it what you want.

Cats

Investing in a cat is a good way to supplement other rodent-proofing methods, while also having the benefit of owning a pet. Once you have gone through the laundry list of ways to prevent rodents from invading your home, you can entertain the idea of purchasing a cat *should* a *minor* problem arise. A cat should not be purchased to stop an existing rodent problem. Cats are not exterminators. Even if you have a mouse scurrying through your home, a cat is not guaranteed to catch it. There are some cats, called mousers, which are experts at nabbing mice. The best mousers are often feral cats, which are the offspring of stray cats that revert back to their wild beginnings as a result of neglect and a lack of human contact. These cats are streetwise and survive on instinct, which means they will attack anything they can eat, anything that scares them, and anything that poses a threat to them. Unfortunately for mice, but fortunately for you, mice represent all three of these situations to feral cats. Of course a cat doesn't have to be feral in order to be a good mouse catcher. There are many cats that just enjoy catching critters and bringing them to their owners. It's almost like a game to them. A way to pass the time away. But then there are some cats who have no interest whatsoever in playing the cat and mouse game. Sheila Klein of Ontario has the art of mouse catching down to a science.

We have four cats. The two older ones were great bird catchers in their time but are not really interested in mice. We got the two younger ones (eighteen months old now) from a cat protection society, and there is a large possibility that their parents were feral or possibly "barn cats." The two younger cats are both male and are great indoor hunters—their front paws are declawed and we try to keep them indoors. They catch and eat flys and bugs and, since January, began catching mice—first just to play with and finally to eat.

We had no idea, when we bought this property a year ago, that mice would be a problem. They get into the house through the basement and have been found on all floors—including in our closet! Believe me, it is no picnic to have a happy cat bounce onto your bed at 3 A.M. with a squeaking present for Mum. The boys were catching four to eight mice a *week* and we finally decided to "assist" them. By the way, these were field mice, dormice, and voles, and boy can they breed fast. We finally bought a sonic emitter about two months ago. Between the cats and the emitter, our basement seems to have undergone a mouse population reversal. Now the boys are down to one mouse—that they fight over—every other week.

Squirrels and Chipmunks

Squirrels and chipmunks are nuts about nuts and will stop at nothing to eat them. This means robbing your walnut trees before you've ever been given the opportunity to taste a home-grown nut, and cleaning out your bird feeder quicker than a bird can chirp. Squirrels have waged war against man, and man has taken the challenge by rising to the occasion. On the one hand, squirrels have made us miserable by pilfering our yards and gardens. But on the other hand, they have challenged us to the point of sheer genius.

Since the focus has been on mice and rats, let's take a moment to discuss the havoc that squirrels wreak in our homes and yards. Gray squirrels and red squirrels like to house themselves in attics. While running around on your roofs, they may come across a hole or a crack and their curious nature takes over. Before you know it, they are in your attic rummaging through your box of winter clothes, and worst of all, nibbling through electrical wires and insulation. Not only can this damage irreplaceable items, but it can also cause fires.

As with all rodent problems, prevention begins with hindering access to your home. Squirrels don't magically appear on your rooftops. They get there via tree branches that are conveniently located near to your home. So trimming nearby tree branches should be your first order of business. When you trim these branches, you have to cut them like you really mean it. Squirrels are good jumpers, so cutting them back four feet away from your home will not suffice. You should make sure that the branches are at least twenty feet away from the building. Your job is to make it more difficult for them to access your home, not invite them in by providing them with a convenient, easy-to-use walkway.

None of the methods used for catching mice and rats are recommended for squirrels. Snap traps, glue boards, poison, and rodenticides are not realistic options. Squirrels are too savvy to walk right into traps, and if one of them gets trapped you can rest assured not too many others will follow. Luckily for them, squirrels will not eat poison. And rodenticides are designed for mice and rats only. This leaves you with only a few conventional options and whatever results of a brainstorming session.

Using live traps to capture squirrels is the traditional option. If you know that you have squirrels in your attic, try placing the trap at the base of your home or a tree, where you know the squirrel will be passing through. Although squirrels love nuts, they are not fragrant enough to attract squirrels to the trap. You must bait the trap with peanut butter or another paste with a nutty base. This does not mean that nuts won't come in handy when baiting the trap. You can still use the nuts as a visual lure, but only in addition to the paste. If you're looking for one of these traps and your local hardware store doesn't have them, the Ketch-All Company offers the 18 Mighty Mite Tru-Catch live trap, which is designed to hold squirrels.

If you're trying to protect a feeder, one option is greasing the feeder's pole. It's as simple as applying WD-40 or any other greasy substance to the pole, and then sitting back to watch squirrels attempt to climb the slippery slope. But be forewarned: persistent and patient squirrels will eventually be able to climb up the pole. Rain, snow, ice, and repeated climbing attempts will cause the grease to be less effective. Teflon in a spray can can also provide temporary relief, in addition to a little comic relief. Although Teflon lasts longer than other oil products, it will eventually come off the pole, dumping you right back onto square one.

If you don't mind making your bird feeder look uninviting, then Nixalite is an avenue you should consider. Nixalite's two- and four-foot-long metal strips featuring 120 razor sharp pinpoints jutting from the strips can be intimidating. The metal strips can be bent to fit any surface and can be reused. Nixalite works by hampering squirrels' attempts to get inside of the bird feeder. Since the squirrel cannot gain solid footing on the pinpoints, or maintain balance on such an unstable surface, it cannot make its way to the entrance, leaving it no choice but to turn around.

Squirrels have a one track mind that is focused on your bird feeder, so that means you need to have a number of tricks up your sleeve. One popular method that is used to stymie their progress is the baffling pole. Because they are popular does not mean that they are consistently effective—they are not. The concept of the baffle is an ingenious one that would be 100 percent effective if squirrels were not so tenacious, determined, and resourceful—but they are. Baffles are put on top of bird feeders to create a ledge that squirrels are unable to navigate, making the bird feeder off limits to them. Think of it as a hat/umbrella/protective gear for the bird feeder. Be sure to pick the largest baffle possible because in this case bigger is certainly better. Also, make sure the bird feeder is as close under the baffle as possible. If you combine a large baffle with good strategic placing, then the chances the squirrel will get the prize are significantly decreased.

Another option is to create a squirrel-proof environment for your birds. You can use a variety of mesh wires, including chicken wire and rubber-coated wire. Using the wire, create a mesh box in which to place the feeder. The key to this squirrel-proof habitat is to make sure the holes of the mesh are large enough for the birds, but too small for the squirrel to enter. Once you create the box, you can use your imagination and make different features for your convenience.

Let's not forget the effect that certain chemicals have on squirrels. The power of cayenne pepper cannot be ignored and should not be overlooked. You can apply cayenne pepper to the pole the same way that you would apply oil to it. Remember to purchase the pepper in liquid form, as it would be a bit of a challenge to smear the powder on the pole and make it stay in place. A strong breeze might render the powder ineffective. GreenMarketplace.com sells Hare Today, Gone Tomorrow Rabbit and Squirrel Repellent, manufactured by Not Tonight Deer. The active ingredients in this spray are capsaicin, capsainoid product, and castor oil. The manufacturers recommend that you spray the feeder as well as the seeds. Don't worry, the spray won't harm birds. You can also use other chemicals, such as a strong menthol cream. Squirrels dislike the smell, texture, and of course, the taste of these products so much that it stops them dead in their tracks when they come in contact with it. The same pitfalls that apply to oil apply to these chemicals: when it rains it's back to the drawing board. This is not a permanent remedy. Also, remember not to rub your eyes after you apply these chemicals. You want to deter or temporarily incapacitate the squirrels, not yourself.

Instead of erecting that hammock you've always wanted between the two trees in your backyard, use the trees to create a pulley system for your bird feeder. You don't have to have trees to do this, you only need two immobile structures. Hook your bird feeder to the pulley and place it between the two structures. Squirrels will have a difficult time accessing the bird feeder, but beware, squirrels are pretty efficient when it comes to walking on a thin line.

As a last resort, you can always compromise. Don't think of it as giving up or giving in, think of it as being diplomatic, an amicable agreement. If the squirrels are entering your home, then you might want to give them the opportunity to live *near* you, just not *with* you by purchasing a squirrel nesting box. If the problem is the squirrel's affinity for your bird feeder, then purchase a squirrel feeder. That way you are feeding the birds, feeding the squirrels, and everybody is content . . . almost.

Porcupines

The second largest rodent in America, the porcupine, is known for its prickly quills. But to those who have been victimized by them, porcupines are known for gnawing and feeding on wood, wooden fixtures, succulent plants, and vegetation, including berries and rosebushes. They also like the taste of salt, so anything that might have salt on it, such as tires, is at risk of being gnawed. During the spring, porcupines feed primarily on available vegetation. When winter rolls around and such vegetation is no longer available, their diets consist largely of bark. While porcupine activity does not kill trees, it can harm them. When porcupines girdle trees (chew the bark off the base of the tree) the trees become weaker and generally more vulnerable. Porcupines are solitary and territorial animals, so they don't take too kindly to relocation programs or any other kind of interference.

Trapping is always an option when it comes to catching rodents, and porcupines are no exception. But catching porcupines can be difficult because they are not easily lured into your live traps. You might want to use a bait with something salty, such as sardines or salt-covered fruit. It is also difficult to locate their dens or the paths they frequent. Be sure to check with state authorities as to whether or not you need a license to use traps, since some states require that you have a license. If you are going to relocate the porcupine after it has been trapped, you need to put a great deal of distance—about twenty to thirty miles—between the porcupine and its former home.

Another way to save the trees is to erect a fence around the trunk of the tree. To make sure that porcupines and beavers don't climb up the fence and gain access to the tree, create a ledge at at least a sixty-degree angle. You can also wrap the trunk of the tree in an aluminum sheet to ward off any potential tree gnawers.

Bears, coyotes, and weasels are among the natural predators that porcupines need to avoid at all costs. In keeping with the hunting theme, porcupines need to watch out for hunters as well. In some areas, porcupine hunting is common because porcupines are edible.

Just as important as knowing what works is knowing what doesn't work. For the most part, repellents do not work on porcupines. There are some repellents on the market, such as Ropel, which is not a poison. It can be sprayed on plants, tools, buildings, or any other object that is being targeted by creatures that like to gnaw. One drawback to using repellents is that they need to be reapplied after less than a month of use. Also, a major rainfall can wash away the Ropel, rendering it ineffective. Another pitfall is that the rodent could develop an immunity to the effects of the repellent, putting you back at square one.

Beavers

Beaver problems can be so serious that some states have programs dedicated to beaver control alternatives. While you are trying to control the beaver population in the problem area, you also need to protect the trees and water levels, so beaver control is often a twofold process.

Let's start off with the usual rodent remedy: traps. Trappers tend to take a more severe approach when it comes to catching beaver. One of the most common traps used is the Conibear 330, which kills the beaver instantly. When a beaver gets caught in one of these traps, it rarely escapes. Because these traps are so lethal, some states prohibit their use on land, allowing them to be used only in water. If you are going to set one of these traps in water, you should use waders or hip boots and come equipped with tongs, or some kind of setting tool, wire, and wire cutters. You should secure the trap with wire so that it is not swept away in the water. For obvious reasons, you should avoid setting these traps with your hands. The trap can be set on top of a beaver dam or right below it. The traps work well when they are set below new dams, and they work even better underneath older ones because the wild vegetation serves as good camouflage. You increase your chances of trapping beavers if you place the traps between the beavers' dens and feeding areas. Also, set up traps at the point where they leave the water to head for land.

Snares are also an option when dealing with beavers. Snares are lighter, more user friendly, and safer for those handling them than the traps. They can be placed in the same area as traps. Snares can be set to spare the life of the beaver, or they can be set to drown it when set in water.

A controversial alternative is the leghold trap. The metal jaws of the trap close down on the leg of the beaver when it steps onto the trap. The degree to which the trap harms beavers, muskrats, and other animals is hotly debated. Some studies indicate that the initial impact of the trap injures the animal, but it is the animal's attempt to set itself free that can cause irreparable damage, such as mutilation to its limbs and tooth loss. On the other hand, there are studies that claim that leghold traps are not as dangerous and harmful as people make them out to be. Some leghold traps are designed to restrain the animal, while others are made to kill them. For instance, the traps can be set to drown the beavers. One problem with these traps is that pets and other unintended victims often get caught in them.

Beavers tend to gravitate toward maple, willow, birch, aspen, alder, and cottonwood. An integral part of beaver control is controlling the actual damage done to natural resources. For instance, you can better your trees' chances of staying healthy by spraying on them repellents such as Ropel or a water and cayenne pepper concoction. Erecting a fence is another option. When selecting wire to make a fence, choose the sturdiest kind. It has to be strong enough to support the weight of a beaver. The fence should be at least four feet high, and should be placed between five to ten inches away from the tree. If the problem is widespread, which is usually the case, erect a fence around a group of trees instead of individually. It is important to keep in mind the severity of the damage beavers can cause to trees and to you. Although beavers do not intend to harm people, persistent gnawing will cause trees to weaken and eventually fall, crashing to the ground. This means that an unsuspecting passerby can be caught off guard and possibly seriously injured.

As for dams, you might want to consider installing devices to regulate the flow of water. Also, if you are planting trees and you know you have beavers in the area, then you should try to plant strategically.

Prairie Dogs

Prairie dogs rely on area vegetation for food and nesting material, and they also clear away nearby brush to eliminate hiding places used by their enemies. They have found an efficient way to use and dispose of available grasses and plants, but that has hurt farmers and ranchers whose livelihood depends on those plants.

Poison and gassing are common options, although their effectiveness depends largely on how much food from natural sources is available. If there is little grass, then the chances that a prairie dog will eat a poison bait are higher than if they have abundant resources. Oat grains treated with poison are a common bait. Since some poisons, such as zinc phosphide, have an unpalatable odor and taste, put down grains that have not been treated with the poison to get the prairie dogs familiar with the bait you are trying to introduce. Once you can confirm that they are eating the untreated grains you can go forward with the poison baits. Fall is a good time to use the poison baits because there are fewer natural resources, and the prairie dogs will be looking for food in preparation for winter.

The Conibear trap is the trap of choice for those trying to rid their lives of prairie dogs. The problems with these traps is that they will not put a dent in a prairie dog population. For smaller colonies, trapping might be a useful option, but for most people who are trying to save farms trapping is too slow a process.

Gardens

All of the aforementioned rodents might make a pit stop in your garden, but it is just a pit stop. They most likely will not clean out your gardens because they are looking for bigger and better foods. They should not be considered a major threat to your carrots, peas, beets, and broccoli. Other rodents, such as the beaver, are not considered major threats to gardens because they are an even greater threat to trees and dam systems. Sometimes you have to choose the lesser of the two evils. What you need to worry about are gophers, voles, and woodchucks. These rodents will not stop digging until they get what they're looking for, which are the contents of your gardens. If you have gophers, voles, or woodchucks in the area—unless you nip the problem in the bud with the following methods—you can kiss your produce good-bye.

Gophers

When dealing with gophers, it is important to get to the root of the problem quickly. This means as soon as you notice that the roots of your plants are being eaten off you need to take action. Not only will you continue to lose plants until a good portion of your garden is wiped out, but you will also be physically at risk. Gophers can make walking in your yard treacherous. Gophers spend most of their time in underground tunnels. As the soil above the tunnels becomes moist, it grows weaker, causing the tunnels to collapse under the pressure of someone walking on it.

A common solution to a gopher problem is a trap. Trapping gophers requires a little more strategy than with other rodents because they spend most of their lives in tunnels. They do their dirty work in the dirt. Locating the mounds that their tunnel systems form is not as challenging because they usually are visible. It is locating the main tunnel that requires patience and attention. Once you locate the mound, dig a circle a little more than a foot away from the mound until you hit the main tunnel. When you find the main tunnel, place the trap in it and wait for an unsuspecting gopher to walk right in. Remember to check your traps daily, if not twice a day. You don't want to make your captive suffer while he awaits relocation. You can order the Black Hole gopher trap from Peaceful Valley Farm Supply. The live trap aims to trick the gopher because it is designed to look like a tunnel with dimensions of 6 ½" × 3 ½".

For those of you who have some extra time on your hands, root guards might be a worthwhile investment. You can purchase them or make them yourselves. Root guards protect roots by forming a cage around the root. If you are making the guard yourself, purchase aviary wire because it has tinier holes. That way the gopher cannot get through it to the root. Pleasant Valley Farm Supply offers the Bulb Gopher Wire Basket, which is a fancy name for a root guard.

Repellents and poison are also options for gopher control. While mothballs emit an odor strong enough to repel gophers, this method should not be mistaken for a cure-all. Putting mothballs in tunnels should be seen as a temporary deterrent. If protecting your landscaping and garden is your top priority, then making your property a gopher-free area should be the goal, and one of the surest ways to do this is to combine methods like trapping and the use of repellents. The most permanent way to wipe out gophers is to use poison, but there is always the issue of animal cruelty as well as the problem of having limited access to the corpse. The animal could die and decay deep in the tunnel, leaving you with a dead animal underground.

Some people use earth vibrators, which are stakes planted in the ground designed to scare away creatures that burrow by sending out shock waves. The jury is out on whether or not this is an effective form of rodent control. There are several factors that affect the effectiveness of these gadgets, including placement and soil type and consistency. If you're on the West Coast, these devices can be found at Handsome Rewards in Perris, California.

Voles

The benefit of having most rodents in your yard is that they are nocturnal. If you have voles on your property, you are not as lucky because they are about and alert night and day. The same beautiful plants and flowers that you showcase around your yard for landscaping are the very same plants, trees, and shrubs that voles damage. Like gophers, voles live in complex tunnel systems, and some utilize runways aboveground. Not only is the vegetation ruined by their feeding activity, but their tunnel systems also disturb water patterns. Voles have been known to girdle trees, which you know from the section on beavers can cause serious damage.

Since voles and gophers have similar feeding and living patterns, many of the methods used to control them are the same, such as tree and root guards, live traps, and poison baits. Snap traps that you would ordinarily use for mice can be used on voles if you have a minor problem. It is not recommended that you use snap traps if you have a vole infestation.

Woodchucks

Woodchucks prefer to reside in open areas, which means that those of you who live on farms or own large acres of land are at risk of being invaded by woodchucks. Farmland is a woodchuck's dream and a farmer's nightmare. Open fields and pastures are also problem areas in terms of woodchuck activity. To give credit where credit is due, it is important to note that their burrowing systems actually improve the condition of soil. But though they have a positive effect on the soil, they have a negative effect on gardens, which is where they love to dine.

Building a fence will not rid you of all of your troubles, but it can reduce greatly the damage done by woodchucks. Keep in mind that woodchucks are expert climbers, and a wire fence is hardly a match for them, so you need to create a fence that even the most athletic woodchuck cannot scale. If you are up to the challenge, purchase the correct amount of wire for a fence and an electric hot-shot wire. To inhibit woodchucks from burrowing underneath the fence, plant the base of the fence at least twelve inches below the surface. Next, install the hot wire on the fence about five inches away from the ground. This will stop any woodchuck right in its tracks.

It is important to consider the time of year when setting out live traps to nab woodchucks. Since woodchucks do hibernate, it would be better to avoid trapping them in late summer, before they begin hibernation. They awaken from their slumber in early summer, so it would be considerate to wait to trap them when they are at their strongest and more prepared. After they have been trapped, set them free in an open area where they have access to a lot of vegetation, especially grass.

For widespread woodchuck problems, drastic measures might be in order. Some people use gas cartridges to rid themselves of these unwanted creatures. First you must seal off entryways to the burrow systems. When all openings are sealed, ignite the cartridge and place it in the burrow. The cylindrical cartridge containing chemicals will burn slowly, emitting carbon monoxide and killing any woodchucks trapped in the burrow. These cartridges are not as easy to find in stores as mice and rat traps, but most farm supply stores carry them.

If you are interested in more creative ways of escorting woodchucks off of your property, stopping the opening of a burrow with a rag soaked in an oil that will turn malodorous as the days go by will drive them out. One way to determine if the problem still persists after using any of these methods is to flatten the mounds, either by stomping on them or using a flat object. If the mounds appear to be disturbed after you have flattened them, then the burrows are active, and woodchucks are present. Woodchucks are excitable creatures, so big animals, like your pet Doberman pinscher, could come in handy. Since they are easily frightened, you might want to use noise to scare them out of their burrows and your yard. Falcon Safety Products, Inc., offers a wide range of handheld horns that just might do the trick. When nothing else works, there are always scare tactics.

6

List of Stratagems

Some of the following methods to stop rodents in their tracks have been used successfully for years. Then there are other strategies that most likely won't work, but they should provide you with a little comic relief while you figure out what methods work best for you. Don't try *all* of these at home.

1. Remove any "Welcome" doormats—they send the wrong message.

2. Play John Tesh albums at the highest volume setting during the day, that way any nocturnal creature within a ten-mile radius will never get any rest and will evacuate the area as soon as possible.

3. Invite a politician to dinner. Some rats like to have a place all to themselves.

4. Have a séance.

5. Make sure all garbage (outdoors and indoors) is tied up in plastic bags and secured in a trash can with a lid.

6. Leave your computer on overnight. Place a snap trap in front of the screen and wait. If you have DSL, they will come.

7. Lock your doors at night.

8. Cough really loudly. Rodents are in contact with enough deadly diseases, they don't need to catch your illness too.

9. Spread word that all of the male rats in your area have been cheating on their ladies. You won't get rid of all of your pests, but some of them won't be coming home tonight.

10. Buy a cat; buy two.

11. Tell your neighbors to stop feeding the rodents.

12. When your children claim they don't have any homework, have them make a list of ways to rid your house of rodents.

13. Go to the pound and bring home the meanest cat. Rodents like to feel at home in your home and a mean cat will drive them away. Note: this might backfire and drive you away.

14. Don't treat pests like pets by providing them room and board.

15. Join Rodent Enablers Anonymous.

16. Place rat traps in rat runways about fifteen to twenty feet apart. Since rats can be equally as cunning, you might have to trick them by plac-ing the trap in a box and cutting an entryway in the side of it. Give it a little time. The rats might

not run for it immediately, but sooner or later they will either become curious or confident and get trapped.

17. Try the first sixteen strategies again. If they don't work, proceed to the next.

18. Don't knock on cabinet doors before you open them. Rodents like their privacy, and they will get tired of you waltzing in on them while they are trying to nibble on the Raisin Bran.

19. Chew bubblegum and make that snapping sound with it. This will alarm nearby rodents, as they will think that the snapping sound is a fellow rodent being caught in a trap.

20. Buy a rat costume and wear it every night when you go to bed.

21. Buy a cat costume and wear it every night when you go to bed.

22. Move to Antarctica—rodents can't stand the cold.

23. Invest in a large pair of dentures modeled after rodent dentition.

24. Place your parents' dentures on top of the rodent traps. Rodents will evacuate quickly, wondering how such a large rat was caught in the trap.

25. Hose your entire house down every week (inside and out).

26. When you spot a mouse, use a blowtorch to scorch it. Either you will scare the mice invading

your house by sending a message, or you will burn down your house—either way you end up without an infestation.

27. Tell your kids not to let strangers into the house.
28. Use caller ID. Some rodents have good manners and like to call before they come.
29. Use a technique crafted by David Ridgeway of Washington, D.C.: Corner the rodent and jab away at it with a steak knife until you can proclaim victory, or until it escapes.
30. If you have hardwood floors, then you should take up tap-dancing. The rats will be driven crazy by the sound of you tap, tap, tapping. Better yet, you might stomp on one while you're pretending to be Fred Astaire.
31. Play Kenny G. while you are out of the house.
32. Leave your child's Pokémon dolls lying around.
33. Leave your child's Beanie Babies lying around.
34. Get rid of all of your worldly goods and live like a true minimalist. This will give the rodents no place to hide.
35. Move all furniture to the middle of the room.
36. Stop eating.
37. Eat out and don't do any more grocery shopping.
38. Cover all exposed floors and counters with shards of glass and poison, then move out.

39. Cover all of your walls with stuffed animals. A taxonomy collection is a surefire way to deter any animal from setting foot in your home.
40. Cover all of the vegetables in your garden with toxic waste.
41. Pave your entire backyard with cement.
42. Place traps under appliances, sinks, and along baseboards.
43. Replace all broken screens.
44. If you have a major mouse infestation, then use multiple-catch traps and kill many mice with one trap.
45. Remove nearby trees that have rats' nests in them.
46. Marry a contractor.
47. Improve your dart-playing skills by practicing on rodents.
48. Don't trust your children when they say that they will make sure the pet gerbil doesn't get away.
49. Leave shoestrings lying around. Since rats have poor eyesight, they will mistake them for rats' tails and head for the hills.
50. Play show tunes from the musical *Cats* over loud-speakers in your yard.
51. Take up archery. Using rodents for target practice is one way to improve your skill.
52. Look on the bright side, you could have a roach infestation.

53. Rig all popular rat hangouts with electric wiring.

54. If you don't want to kill the mouse, instead of laying down poison, use a muscle relaxant. This will slow them down a bit and you will be able to catch them any way you wish.

55. Limit the food supply in and around your homes. This will serve as a deterrent to most rodents because food is what they are looking for in the first place.

56. If you have a porcupine problem, treat the targeted plants and materials with Ropel, which is an odorless, liquid repellent. Ropel works because it tastes horrible. One application generally lasts for about three weeks to a month. If you plan on spraying fruits and vegetables, try to avoid spraying parts of the plant you want to eat, because it will affect the taste.

57. Invest in a lot of gloves, disinfectant, and plastic bags if you have a rat or mouse infestation. When you start catching rodents, you'll need them.

58. If you have minor mouse problem and a little time on your hands, use the umbrella method. You will need an umbrella, a partner, a pair of running shoes, a magazine, and a good sense of humor. Once you spot the mouse, alert your partner, who should have an open umbrella ready. Steer the mouse in the direction of the open umbrella by holding the open magazine

behind it, giving it nowhere to run but toward the umbrella. Once the mouse runs into the umbrella, the person holding it should close it and tie it shut. Then dispose of it as you like.

59. Use ultrasonic devices as rodent repellents. Rodents are very sensitive to the sounds emitted from them.

60. Remember, never use one snap trap or glue trap, even if you think you have a minor problem. The fewer you use, the less your chances are of nabbing the critter.

61. Hire a contractor to cement your backyard. This will give rodents no place to burrow.

62. Purchase the larger size snap traps when you are treating a rat problem. The smaller sizes are designed for mice and are too small for rats. They will just end up dragging those traps throughout your home.

63. Put explosives and other flammable articles in burrows and then sit back and watch the fireworks. This is a surefire way to get rid of big burrowers, like prairie dogs and chipmunks.

64. If the traps don't appear to be working, move the furniture around. Since mice are curious by nature, they will wander around investigating, increasing their chances of stumbling upon a trap.

65. For a short-term solution, pour gasoline into chipmunk burrows. This will drive them out of

the immediate area, but they will probably relocate.

66. To protect your gardens from pocket gophers, use root guards. You can either purchase root guards, which form a protective shield around plant roots, or you can use chicken wire to make your own barrier.

67. Give beavers less work to do by installing devices yourself to regulate the flow of water. That way beavers won't feel the need to take it upon themselves to do so.

68. Keep your soil damp and moist. Wet soil is difficult for gophers to dig. Also wet soil will hold noxious gas, emitting it in tunnels.

69. Use baffles on your bird feeders to hinder access to them by squirrels.

70. Purchase an earth vibrator to scare away underground dwellers. These stakes are put into the ground and send out shock waves.

71. To save trees from damage caused by busy beavers, invest in spray-on products.

72. Do yourself a favor and don't plant your prized trees around a beaver pond.

73. If squirrels are intent on getting closer and closer to your home, put a squirrel nesting box on a nearby tree. They'll find it very comforting, and you'll find it convenient.

74. Purchase a squirrel feeder to protect your bird feeder.

75. Keep branches trimmed back from your home so that squirrels don't gain easy access to your home.

76. Elevate your woodpiles at least fifteen inches off the ground to keep mice from burrowing underneath it.

77. Use mothballs as a rodent deterrent. These can be used in a number of areas where you know rodent activity is taking place.

78. Repair or cover all openings to your home with concrete, hardware cloth, brick, aluminum, perforated sheet metal grills, or galvanized sheet metal.

79. Put a seed catcher beneath your bird feeder.

80. Purchase a tokay gecko.

81. Purchase a metal trash can instead of a vinyl or plastic one, as rodents can gnaw through them easily.

82. Trim all brush at least three feet back from the side of your home. Exposed areas discourage rodent activity.

83. Eliminate all sources of water. This is essential, especially when dealing with a rat problem.

84. Erect a nonwood fence around trees about twelve inches from the tree to keep beavers at bay.

85. Put snap traps on a piece of cardboard to increase the surface area of the trap and your chances of catching a mouse or rat.

86. Invest in Tupperware stock. Using Tupperware is the best way to make sure rats and mice can't get into your food. They will nibble through almost all other forms of containers.

87. Purchase a pulley for your bird feeder. This device will enable you to put the feeder in an area between two immobile structures that squirrels will have difficulty accessing.

88. Grease bird feeder poles and watch squirrels attempt to climb them unsuccessfully.

89. Mice are not fans of peppermint oil, so apply some to cotton balls and place it in suspected entryways.

90. If you are desperate and nothing else has worked, use poison to put mice and rats out of commission.

91. Use gummy, sticky substances as bait to ensure that the trap is set off while the rodent tugs at the bait.

92. Nix squirrels with Nixalite.

93. Stop feeding birds in your backyard or even in public areas.

94. Learn to be more of an opportunist than rodents are.

95. Go to the pound and pick out the meanest feral cats you can find.

96. Heat things up by sprinkling a little cayenne pepper on the pole of your bird feeder.

97. Line fences with hot wire to deter woodchucks from scaling fences.

98. Plug woodchuck burrows with olive oil–soaked rags.

99. Get a complete list of the animals that prey on your rodent, then introduce them to your environment.

100. Try the first ninety-nine over again. One of them is bound to work.

7

Products

Woodstream Corporation
P.O. Box 327
69 North Locust Street
Lititz, PA 17543
800-800-1819

Havahart Products
www.havahart.com

Havahart.com offers a number of remedies to various pest problems, including mice, moles, raccoons, rabbits, skunks, squirrels, deer, and groundhogs. Their signature is "Caring Control for Pets and Wildlife," and they provide solutions in the form of live-catch traps, animal training products, and pest-proof products. For mice, this site offers a number of options, including the line of Victor live-catch mouse traps and snap, the Victor Pest Chaser, among others. This site also has a fairly detailed list of solutions.

Handsome Rewards
19465 Brennan Avenue
Perris, CA 92379
909-943-2023

Handsome Rewards offers a line of vibrating stakes, which you could use if the stakes aren't too high.

The Ketch-All Company
4149 Santa Fe Road #2
San Luis Obispo, CA 93401
805-543-7223
www.ketch-all.com

This Web site offers a wide range of traps for a wide range of pests. Some of these Tru-Catch traps are designed to trap squirrels and other small animals.

Peaceful Valley Farm Supply
P.O. Box 2209
Grass Valley, CA 95945
916-272-4769
www.groworganic.com

Peaceful Valley Farm Supply's Web site is both user friendly and extensive. They offer over 320 weed and pest management products, 14 of which are specifically for rodents. Rodent management products include mouse and rat bait and spiral tree guards. There are even urine darts, which help create the illusion that predators are in the area. They sell locally in their retail store and nationwide via mail, phone, fax. On-line ordering is available.

Reed-Joseph International Company
P.O. Box 894
Greenville, MS 38702
601-335-5822
800-647-5554
www.reedjoseph.com

The Web site features Reed Joseph International's accumulated expertise of forty-five years of bird and wildlife control. The company is known for using sound and movement to disperse animal and wildlife pests from urban and agricultural environments. In another gesture of environmental responsibility, before Reed-Joseph International will fill any order you must have a wildlife control statement on file, ensuring that their products will be used in a safe and responsible manner. Their technicians are available for free consultation.

Falcon Safety Products, Inc.
1065 Briston Road
Mountainside, NJ 07092
201-233-5000
www.falconsafety.com

This company does not specialize in pest management, but it is the leader in handheld signal horns. This means that if you are looking to rid your life or rodents through the use of noise, then you have found the right place.

Nixalite of America, Inc.
1025 Sixteenth Avenue
East Moline, IL 61244
309-755-8771
fax: 309-755-0077
www.nixalite.com

Nixalite specializes in bird control, but some of their products, such as their line of copper mesh, may also be useful for those of you plagued by rodents. You can e-mail questions or comments to birdcontrol@nixalite.com or call toll-free 888-624-1189.

Pioneer Wildlife Control
P.O. Box 307
Westwood, MA 02090
860-774-5034 or 413-783-4462
www.pioneerwildlife.com/pioneerwildlife.html

Pioneer Wildlife Control prides itself on humanely resolving wildlife damage and managing pests through exclusion and removal technology. Exclusion is a process in which the offending animal is evicted from your home unharmed. The company does not use any chemicals, except on rare occasions when repellents are absolutely necessary. Pioneer Wildlife Control stresses that exclusion is better than trapping, because trapping, by law, requires you to relocate the animal, a practice that is forbidden in certain states.

Animaltraps.com
800-476-3368
www.animaltraps.com/index.html

Animaltraps.com offers traps for rats, mice, squirrels, raccoons, opossums, and moles. Their product line includes live cages, glue traps, multiple traps, and snap traps. Along with this, they have a list of suggested baits for your particular pest. Animaltraps.com also offers links to other useful Web sites.

Seventh Generation
One Mill Street
Box A26
Burlington, VT 05401
802-658-3773
fax: 802-658-1771
www.seventhgen.com

Seventh Generation is a great company to turn to if you are looking for pest repellents (such as hot capsaicin) that are truly environmentally safe. Their mission is to provide high-quality nontoxic and environmentally responsible products to their customers. The company even derives its name from the Iroquois belief that "in our every deliberation, we should consider the impact of our decisions on the next seven generations." But beware that while environmentally friendly, this company does not specialize in pest control, so selection may be limited. On-line shopping is available. GreenMarketplace sells several natural alternatives to pest control such as pepper repellents.

Med-Pest Control
350 Mountain Avenue
Middlesex, NJ 08846
732-469-5999
fax: 732-271-1824
www.medpest.com

Med-Pest Control and Supply offers a variety of products, ranging from zappers to baits to traps to repellents. The Web site also gives some useful information on illnesses contracted from rodents, including symptoms and what to do about them.

References

The following sources are useful for learning more about rodents:

Alderton, David. *A Petkeeper's Guide to Hamsters & Gerbils.* London, England: Salamander Books, 1996.

————. *Rodents of the World.* Poole, England: Blandford, 1999.

Miller, Sara Swan. *Rodents from Mice to Muskrats.* New York: Franklin Watts, 1998.

Sterry, Paul. *Beavers and Other Rodents.* New York: Todtri Productions, Ltd., 1998.

Index